THE AIRBNB EQUATION

The Ultimate Insider Guide in the New Age of
Capitalism- And how to build a portfolio of
Airbnb Properties with "No Money Down"

TERRENCE HOOI

CONTENTS

Chapter I: The New Capitalists of the Sharing Economy

Chapter II: The Rise of Airbnb

Chapter III: From Actor to Hotel Kingpin

Chapter IV: Running a Hotel Empire from the Beach

Chapter V: Global Mega Disruption

Chapter VI: Difference Between Money, Wealth and Status

Chapter VII: Why the money in your Bank Account is Losing Value

Chapter VIII Schelling point in Business and Airbnb Listings

Chapter IX: It's a Winner Take All Game in the Innovation Economy

PUBLISHERS DISCLAIMER

This book presents a wide range of options about a variety of topics related to the innovation economy which is ever changing, including certain ideas, and procedures that may be illegal in some geographic locations without proper legal consultation. These opinions reflect the research and ideas of the author or those who ideas the author presents, but are not intended to substitute for the services of legal and regulatory laws of the city you live in When deciding whether to use the ideas presented in this book, it's important for you to understand how the laws work in your city.

In many cities, these rules can be confusing, and in some tax jurisdictions, Airbnb is still working with governments around the world to clarify these rules. The Airbnb Equation is not a registered investment, legal or tax advisor or a broker/dealer. All investment expressed in this book are from the personal research and experience of the owner of the site and are intended as educational or entertainment purposes only. Although best efforts are made to ensure that all information is accurate and up to date, occasionally unintended error and misprints may occur.

TERRENCE'S DISLAIMER

Risk is fundamental to the investment process. It's very important to do your own analysis before making any investment based on your own personal circumstances.

To all my "new capitalist companions on the path," may you be a force for good in this world and see the same in yourselves.

-Terrence

CHAPTER I: THE NEW CAPITALISTS OF THE SHARING ECONOMY

The New Wealth is made by code, the last generations of wealth was made by capital -the Warren Buffetts and Rockefellers of the world. Now you can generate passive income from a portfolio of virtual properties combining all these three, one year lease, good location with an internet connection.

The Sharing Economy's newest capitalists represents a unique and unconventional breed of new rich. A new breed of entrepreneurs riding the massive wave of the sharing economy and generating a consistent passive income leveraging on the permission-less economy. In the innovation economy, technology move so quickly, and if you are not thinking about whats next, the world around you change faster than you do.

Not too long ago, buying a house, owning a car and the concept of having several possessions was the pinnacle of "making it" in life. But in the permission-less economy, less is more. The idea of sharing an asset has now becoming a norm and leaving ownership behind. Underutilized assets from cars to now properties are abundantly available with the help of technology. Smart capitalist have begun to figure out how to turn under utilized resources into money and reduce the cost burden of ownership. According to Forbes, the sharing economy is projected to grow from $15 billion in 2014 to $355 billion in 2025. Quicker than ever, we're shifting into a world of shared economy.

So how does the new age of capitalist survive or even thrive in this ever-changing innovation economy? It's part of being a pioneer and it's not just exciting to build a portfolio of cash generating assets but to explore new fields and to recognize what comes with that is a lot of upside potential capturing the wave of sharing economy. What separates the new capitalists can be characterized by options. Traditional property investors, those who sati it all for the end only to find that life has passed them by. The New Capitalist can be separated from the traditional investing principles based on their goals. To think big but ensure payday comes ever day. Cash flow first, big payday second.

With the advent of smartphones, these new age of capitalists or property owners are building the portfolio of cash flow positive properties around the world. The playbook of the Airbnb Equation will let you gain unique insider access to today's most influential sharing economy entrepreneurs, creating businesses, even with no coding skills, build a consistent stream of passive income.

In this new information age, you should think like the new rich, because you do not need permission from large corporations anymore. Your business will torpedo the backup industry, if you do it right, all within one to three years. You now have the power to create streams of cash flows by building a portfolio of properties accessible by the millions of people who've bought iPhones, iPads, or even a desktop computer connected to the ever increasing bandwidth speed. Imagine you have guests coming in from London, Berlin, Japan staying in your list of properties and then going back to where they came from, thats the kind of business we are trying to build in this sharing economy.

Unlike the Warren Buffetts and hedge fund managers in the previous decade, the new rich have conjured their millions if not billions without having much capital to start with.

First time property investors tend to ricochet between these two anxieties, fear of losing money and fear of missing out. Airbnb's success suggested that an overabundance of caution in the dawning sharing economy fueled by the digital age. But it wasn't so easy for property investors a decade ago to find and purchase a property for the purpose of generating a passive income.

Now familiar with the headache of saving up for a downpayment and servicing the mortgage every month, conventional property investors were taking longer to break even and generate positive cash flow from properties. The flood of millennials into staying at short term rentals in the year following Airbnb's resurgence spawned more property owners to list their properties that can potentially generate 300-500% more than income compared to traditional leasing option.

In a span of just six months, the new age of capitalist like Linda has built a portfolio of 10 Airbnb properties in Singapore generating more than $25,000 per month in passive income. These were eye-popping numbers conventional property owners had never seen before especially for first time property investor like Linda who owns no real estate. The sharing economy explosive growth has astounded even optimistic market pundits.

Relative Income vs. Absolute Income

So what's the difference between relative income and absolute income? Tim Ferris from the 4 hour work week explained absolute income is measured using one and only variable- the dollar amount you make. Say John Doe makes $100,000 per years and Suzie makes $50,000 per year, this makes John twice as rich as

Suzie.

But Relative Income is different. It is measured with two variables. Dollar and time. It measure per hour income. When using relative income, let's use the previous example of John making $100,000 per year for 60 weeks per year and works 100 hours per week. John makes $17 per hour. Suzie on the other hand, makes $50,000 per year, working 20 hours per week for 60 weeks per year. Suzie makes $42 per hour. In relative income, Suzie is 2.5 times richer.

The sharing concept isn't new. Rentable assets have been around for ages. The sharing economy has redefined the way we think about services, belongings, and property, creating a new economic model which will enrich those who know how to capitalize on this wave. In 1995, eBay kick started the sharing economy providing a global online marketplace where anyone could list and sell just about any kind of item. eBay was the first 24/7 platform which enables people with huge selection of stock from retailers ti seek at competitive prices. The second wave of sharing economy companies like Airbnb and Uber proved to be a bigger wave enabling entrepreneurs to build businesses all around the world.

eBay enabled entrepreneurial retailers to build businesses and buying and reselling products at a premium reaching a global audience of shoppers from their home. Now with Airbnb, you could also build a sizable business with portfolio of properties all around the world, letting travelers to find and book from one of your listings 24/7. These platforms have provided easy access to a whole new "no money down" opportunity to anyone with an internet connection, making for a more interconnected communities of individuals that are able to pay you in cash on a daily basis.

If a right pricing and niche is found, you can have an incredibly low risk while generating a consistent monthly income that often have more variety compared to traditional hotel chains. Just like Airbnb owns no properties, and hasn't built a single home since its inception over a decade ago, entrepreneurs in the sharing economy can capitalize on this wave and be one of the pioneers of sharing economy 2.0, a massive global industry, which is projected to grow into $335 billion by 2025.

Folks outside the property industry, people from all walks of life are feeling left out. People want to know how to grab a share a the pie from the permission-less economy. People want to solve their money problems but everyone vaguely knows that they want to be wealthy but they don't have the right set of principles to achieve that.

What we are seeing in the digital economy is that structural changes in consumer behavior or in traditional retail have changed a lot in the past decades. What we see unfolding in the hotel industry is a form of insanity. Airbnb is now bigger than the world's top five hotel brands put together. On any given night, 2 million people are staying in other people's home around the world on Airbnb.

CHAPTER II: THE RISE OF AIRBNB

According to Business Insider, Airbnb has grown into 191 countries – outstrips Marriott International, Hilton Worldwide, Intercontinental Hotel Group, Wyndham Worldwide and Accor Hotel Group, which have 3.9 m listings between them. With internet and smartphone penetration growing rapidly around the world, your portfolio of listing is enticing to travelers and irresistible to business people looking for a short term stay.

If conventional way of buying a property and renting it out to tenants, keep applying what doesn't work, and when that fails, do it some more. That's the definition of insanity. We all know people who frequently lament their decision to invest in real estate. They believe the entire process is predicated on luck and timing, an exercise in chance.

Whether you are losing money investing, it's easy to blame the market, or real estate as an industry. While no investment is without risk, the new age of capitalist understand there are certainly patterns that can be capitalized and pitfalls to be avoided to mitigate that risk. In more than a decade of investing in tech companies in the world *Tesla, Uber, Netflix, Apple, Twillio* and 30+ more. I've found patterns in the stock markets what went well, and I've also seen patterns in the sharing economy and in creating optionality in the business world and also in trading the financial markets. In other words, I've found patterns that went well and I've also seen patterns that don't work at all.

Airbnb would emerge from this conflagration of capital with conviction as the giants of the new era of sharing economy is the new norm. By the start of 2014, Airbnb has raised $320 million in venture capital and was valued by investors at $2.5 billion. By 2019, Airbnb has raised a total of $4.7 billion led by Fidelity Investments, BlackRock and now Wall Street is desperate to capitalize on the success of Airbnb for global supremacy.

As Airbnb swelled in size, value and ambition, traditional hotel operators around the world grew increasingly concerned about their businesses. For Airbnb, anyone could list their properties, and generate an income from it. Did the benefits of Airbnb's dominance help you as a new capitalist in this new wave of sharing economy? How many days do I need to list out to cover the monthly rental? Does the benefits of leasing outweighs buying the property outright? Facing these questions, I have to shed the baggage of my pasts failed attempts to generate income from properties, would have to rise to meet the future of property investing.

CHAPTER III: FROM ACTOR TO HOTEL KINGPIN

I was intrigued by the idea of 'no money down' property investing deals but wanted reassurances that I could cover the monthly mortgage. The truth is, with traditional leasing options, the math still amounts to negative cash flow every month. So one evening in August 2016, I checked into a suite at the Fullerton Hotel in downtown Singapore, paid for by my company, and woke up the next morning for a nine o'clock breakfast meeting with the smartest man who capitalized on the sharing economy. When I came down to the lobby, a man with hawaiian shirt and shorts sat in the town restaurant table. It was my first epiphany in leveraging the sharing economy with little or no capital.

At the coffee lounge, Chan showed me that the playbook could work together to built a portfolio of global Airbnb properties, which the new rich relied on for consistent cash flows every week, but he didn't say much or stay very long. The more important legacy that day was me developing awareness of the system that might radically change property investing.

His name was Robert Chan who was a native San Franciscan whose parents emigrated from China, Chan went to Columbia University as a math major and then made millions trading government securities on Wall Street at Citibank. After seven years,

Robert found that the Wall Street life was too constraining so he decided to reinvent himself by dropping the name Robert in favor of Toshi became an actor for The Departed, Collateral Beauty and Daredevil. At the age of twenty five, he added "With my masters of the Universe ego on Wall Street, I thought "If I can trade billions, I don't see how hard it can be for me to win an Academy Award." "Toshi" and became famous for over-the-top parties a few times a year for a series of elaborate "Toshi Parties" at the Puck Building in SoHo and he used this Wall Street winnings to buy a four-story former yeshiva on a quiet street in south Williamsburg and renovated the entire structure by adding a two-two-flow penthouse with high ceilings.

With acting jobs sporadic and a non consistent income, Chan quickly find himself under employed. His wife Cha Chang, recalled months Chan would rent our one of the guest rooms in his penthouse for a few weeks posting it on Craigslist for hundred and fifty dollars a night.

With the rise of sharing economy and Airbnb, a smart capitalist like Chan quickly saw the opportunity to list his apartment on the internet, charge tourists one hundred and fifty per night and if he rented his guest room for twenty days in a month, he would make three thousand dollars from one room alone. Very soon, he began listing apartments in the six floor building next door, which he leased on favorable terms from the landlord. Whether it is tourists or business travelers, start flocking in from the airport into their short term apartment picking up their keys. His then fiancee, Cha Chang even invented a breakfast menu, charing five dollars for eggs or suggesting nearby diners.

The woes of real estate started to deepen in 2008, landlords today struggle with paying their bills.
This was Chan's opportunity, signing and annual leas on a dozen of cheap two-bedroom apartments around the corner and post them on Craigslist. In 2008, Airbnb did not exist, Chan expanded creating his own website hoteltoshi.com, and turned to

tourism services like feelnyc.com which is hugely popular in Europe and Roomorama, a New York-focused apartment rental site which opened the same year. When Cha Chang read about an online article about Air Bed and Breakfast, they added that to their listing options.

In 2009, Airbnb was still in an incubator called Y Combinator. Chan began to communicate with one of the co founders of Airbnb, Brian Chesky. Chesky proposed he could pay twenty-nine dollars a years and upgrade to premium membership that allows host like chan to list properties that are priced over three hundred dollars a night. Chesky also wrote in a email explained in the cook The UpStarts "Many of our premium listers are our best hosts." Followed by "I would be happy to talk to you about this, and arrange something that works for you. How many listings are you looking to post?"

As the financial crises and the stock markets took a hit, Chan made even more aggressive expansion plans. He found a co-investor who signed leases for some two hundreds other apartments across Brooklyn and on Manhattan's Upper West Side. He even had a tent and a queen sized bed on the roof of this penthouse and rented it out on Airbnb for a hundred dollars a night and Daily News reporters wrote about his story.

As his Airbnb passive income grew, Chan moved his office from his home into the basement of a nearby building in Williamsburge, where he rented about half of the thirty-five units. He even hired bike messengers to send their keys to and with cartoon logo of him, to meet guests at their apartments. Although orchestrating check-ins and changing clean sheets every was a nightmare, it didn't stop him from managing a portfolio of thirty five units. He recalled "The worst part was the incessant, shrieking phone calls from the permanent residents of the buildings, who were understandably livid about the nonstop tourist traffic and late-night partying by guests.

To a certain point, Hotel Toshi was hiring more than hundred employees and it gained the attention of Major Michael Bloomberg who suspected the operation was of dubious legality. By 2009, the landlords and a group of apartment-listing websites organized a protest at city hall. Even Airbnb's co-founder Joe Gebbia flew to New York to attend the event.

Chan recalls reclining on his couch from the penthouse of the Flatiron Hotel on the corner of Twenty-Sixth and Broadway in Manhattan, "I went from making five thousand a month to twelve million a month in just a couple of years." He added. "It was crazy".

I Ubered home that night to my Airbnb, near City Central in Singapore. Once back, I received a frantic phone call from my host, who I had never met in person (he was on vacation but left me the keys) to make sure I was okay. The next morning, he messaged me on Airbnb: " I was relieved to hear you checked in and everything was okay yesterday. Hope you have a great week despite a busy holiday week in Singapore."

It was no doubt one of the simple acts of kindness and the sort of unquantifiable variable founders that make Airbnb's impact a global political calculation in low trust society we live in today.

But why is now the time to capitalize on building your Airbnb hotel empire? Before 2017, Airbnb were facing many battles all around the world despite small victories. In 2016, the city of Berlin decided to ban all landlords from letting their apartments to shot-term visitors, enforced by a maximum of $123,000 fine. Citizens were asked to report violaters renting their premises out for vacation rentals and the fine is intended as a menacing message to anyone tempted to reserve an apartment as a full-time vacation let.

The same year, Japan frozen a huge portion of home listings on

Airbnb, about 62,000 homes, apartments, and rooms have been removed from the site, leaving around 13,800 on the site. A new Japanese law called *Minpaku* to address the contemporary rental market. Bottomline, the hotel industry had very serious concerns about the impact disruptive technologies like Airbnb will have.

In June 2016, San Francisco requires host to register to meet its requirements to offer temporary rentals. And the same month, New York State legislature passed a bill that argued Airbnb people tried to exploit the service. Airbnb filed another lawsuit in federal court against general Eric Schneiderman, Mayor Bill de Blasio and the City of New York.

After three years of debate from Barcelona to Santa Monica, regulators attempted rein in Airbnb and its competitors with regulations is not stopping user growth from doubling every year. Even if regulators decided to fight with tech-enabled platform like Airbnb, one major challenge remains. How do they find and monitor illegal rentals? Traditional code of enforcement like door knocking and taking photos have been supplanted with 'web scrapes' and other high-tech approaches on platform like Airbnb.

With Airbnb's $4.4 Billion in funding to build a data-driven platform, "it's like bringing a knife to a gun fight." Although the U.S District Court upheld San Francisco's ability to list on Airbnb, the fines will be imposed with a fine, and there are still myriad ways for hosts to elude the cities' regulatory efforts. Airbnb saw this as good-faith effort to tailor its business to the housing realities of big cities. San Francisco has been held up as a regulatory success story after its ruling were updated in 2017. Since the tougher enforcement regime was put in place especially in San Francisco and New York City, the sizable growth in listings of units continues to rise all around the world.

As new investors continued to fund Airbnb with bigger valuations and more employees, by mid 2016 Airbnb has twenty-six hundred employees. Inside Airbnb, departments have doubled or tripled in size with the frantic rhythm of relentless growth. Airbnb's Nulty counters the number of lawsuits that Airbnb has brought is small relative to the 88,000 cities where the platform operates. He also added "With New York's desire to have unfettered access to host data without due process, these were unmistakable signs of the company shedding its identity as a startup and marching toward an eventual IPO.

CHAPTER IV: RUNNING A HOTEL EMPIRE FROM THE BEACH

An opportunist like Gene Dexter who operates more than seven homes in Southern California, Phoenix, Detroit, Las Vegas, New Orleans, Panama, Seattle and Thailand making more than 7 figures per month, he takes great pride in carefully designing each of his units with items from his travels. He said that tougher regulations in a city would be a major factor in his deciding where to operate, "they are kind of cool challenge for me". "With tech-enabled platform like Airbnb, I could easily play the game to the point where- catch me if you can".

In the near future, I foresee a need for policy-makers and sharing economy platforms like Airbnb to work together, and that outdated rules and policies would prove a sticking point. To date, there is no city that has "figured it out" or developed a fully integrated strategy, although some cities has issued a declaration of common principles and commitment for sharing cities.

Beyond 2020, this momentum is like to continue. Whether it is genuine inter-city outcome or implementation or collective negotiation, it remains to be seen.

With the use of the internet, entrepreneurs like Toshi also ran online ad campaigns during these early years. If people searched Google for an apartment in Boston, for example, his property would pop up linking to his listing on Airbnb. Toshi and his marketing team became experts at finding the cheapest leases and empty properties and generating a crisp and somewhat pointed ads to his website and then to Airbnb. Toshi pioneered a clever use of Facebook's fledging ad system, which allows companies to tailor and target ads to the interests and hobbies that members specified in their profiles. For example, if there is an upcoming Annual Conference in New York City, attendees interested in going to the event would see an ad of one of Toshi's listings from Airbnb that says "Rent an entire Condo an NYC Central Park before Annual Developer Hackathon".

Facebook ads are cheap and people tended to respond to these eerily targeted messages. Those Facebook ads worked beautifully and powered the listing owner's expansion. When Hotel Toshi quietly grown into a popular destination for international tourists to stay in Brooklyn, at its peak making more than $1 million dollars a month turning Toshi Chan went from actor to hotel Kingpin, operating with more than 18 buildings in New York City where his company operates. Chan realized he had to make customer service a priority.

CHAPTER V: GLOBAL MEGA DISRUPTION

The buzzword today is disruption. But what is getting disrupted really? True disruption can come from unexpected angles in this innovation economy. Airbnb for example is now bigger than the world's top five hotel brands with 4 million listings on their site, outstripping *Marriott International, Hilton World, Intercontinental Hotel Group, Wyndham Worldwide* and *Accor Hotel Group* with only 3.9 Million. Airbnb claims to have 2 million people staying in their listed properties every single day all around the world.

While traditional corporations are playing catch up, startups continue to move fast and upend the rules of this new age of capitalism. There are countless examples we can give you but the pattern is always the same. When *Netflix* execs Marc Randolph and Reed Hastings met with Blockbuster brass in 2000 offering them to buy Netflix for $50 Million, Blockbuster laughed them out of the room. Today, Netflix is worth over $129 Billion, meaning if you had invested in Netflix, you would have made 25 times your money today. Perhaps, Reed was struggling not to laugh today as Blockbuster was driven out of the marketplace.

It reminds one of the medicine practices centuries ago where doctors would let patients bleed. The worse they got, the more they were bled. This all the more reason to adapt in this digital economy and which is holding back most corporate investments. Businesspeople in the new digital age need to know what the rules are before they commit, what's driving the innovation economy and huge success may provide a teachable moment to your floundering competitors in your industry.

Don't get me wrong, I'm not writing this book to challenge the hotel industry or regulators. Every great startup I believe starts as a side project that isn't anybody's main priority. Most Airbnb hosts started listing their extra room as a way to pay their rents. For me, it was a way to experiment with a passive cash flow business model so that it can buy me more time to help me scale it into a big business.

In fact, investing to generate cash flow from properties in this age requires a very different understanding as everything is always in a flux in this innovation economy. We must open ourselves to a wide spectrum of opportunities, we must test various business models; we must learn to appreciate the laws of branding. One of the best ways to thrive in the innovation economy is to break free from competition.

In most developed countries, or at least fluid societies where anyone of any race could quickly turn from rags to riches, the great majority in most human societies have access to education. In truth, young people today are suffering from depression than ever.

We have more products than older generations, the automobile, the smartphone, and of course the internet. We have been sold by the largest corporations in the world that we are not good enough. Every *Apple* ads every six months to a year comes with the same pseudoscientific approach to careful crafted messages like unprecedented leap in …, better than ever…, world's most popular this … or that… for the first time ever…like never before… and so on.

The world is spending billions daily to tell us one thing. That we are not good enough. And in order to be happy we must consume as many products and services as possible. If we feel not quite right or something missing, it's time to visit the nearest car dealership and pick up that brand new car, or that new dress, or that designer bag or cheeseburgers. Every channels from television to your smartphone screen claiming that consumerism will make your life better. But that worked massively well when it comes to baby boomers. Millennials would rather spend money on experiences than on things.

Millenials soon realized brands are trying to sell to all consumers and there is never enough with endless products that we don't really need, at least not until today that we didn't know exist.

As millennials get older, which will most likely be your main target market, their salaries increase, and many consumer brands are finding it hard sell millennials things. Spending habits of millennials believe that spending money on experiences can create a longer-lasting, more substantial payoff, according to financial expert Jean Chatzky. Think of your last vacation experience, it not only created memories but also anticipation. Studies by JPMorgan has shown that millennials are willing to pay more for things such as travel, entertainment, and dining compared to their parents and grandparents.

Why the travel industry is "recession proof"

The package tour industry and tour operators found that customers will still refuse to give-up their holiday abroad even during the credit crunch has hit other industries in 2008. Vacations remain a priority and many industry experts claim that the travel industry is "recession proof".

This can even be traced going back to 1990 during a stock market crash that vacations are one of the last things consumers cut back on. The travel industry continues to be strong in all major markets with robust consumer demand. Peter Long, TUI's chief executive calling the sector "recession proof, I don't believe the industry is cyclical." The first is the rise in oil prices, now the rise of low-cost airlines meaning short term rental platforms like Airbnb is not the only industry to stand firm if there is a recession in the next five years.

Thomas Jefferson drafted the American Declaration of Independence that every person has the right to "Life, Liberty and the pursuit of Happiness". Happiness can mean different thing to different person. Pleasure of buying things can be fleeting and even billionaires experience same pain like normal people do, billionaires get sick and die. But millennials might be getting something right when it comes to their spending habits and here's why:

1.) EXPERIENCE GET BETTER WITH TIME

When you experience something, you make memories. You could go back to the photos on your smartphone today and revisit, which brings the original burst of happiness you felt in the moment back to the fore. With the influence of social media, affluent millennials prioritize their experiences on social and at the same time seeking some form of validation. What if one of your Airbnb tenants shared your chic one bedroom apartment to her 50k followers?

2.) ANTICIPATION OF EXPERIENCE LEADS TO MORE HAPPINESS

The social aspect of anticipation of the experience leads to more happiness and joy. Studies found that some people travel to include other people like loved ones or family members to strengthen relationships.

3.) EXPERIENCES INVOLVE PHYSICAL ACTIVITY

Traveling can make you stronger, both physically and emotionally. In the short term, spending money on traveling can boost physical well being while reducing stress. Traveling involve more physical activity whether its walking from the airport or in your hotel bedroom with a partner. It the long term, you will be more able to handle stresses in life which in turn make your stronger. Think also the willingness of millennials splurging on pricey $30 *Soulcycle* spin classes. For many millenials, they understand the long-term benefits they reap by making the upfront cost of travelling. Data-driven platforms like Airbnb allow you as the owner to know that by compiling all of your customers profile and reason for booking.

According to research, comfort is often more enjoyable than excess. Nagpaul and Pang in their studies about materialism found that "materialism lowers well-being". They explained materialistic pursuits are extrinsic, in pursuit of social position, status and identity. They also found that individuals who buy luxury products experienced less of a sense of autonomy and greater degree of negative affect. The reason, materialistic thoughts caused them to make upward social comparisons, or "keeping up with the Joneses' comparing themselves who have more possessions and higher status.

Once they found they could not afford the latest limited edition ten thousand dollars designer handbag because their friend is carrying one, it leads to decreased sense of autonomy, and an increased sense of self disatisfaction anxiety, and distress.

BUYING LOVED ONES A VACATION, NOT SOCIAL COMPARISON

Aknin et al suggested that spending choices have a greater impact on well-being. Aknin pointed that experiences provide more enjoyment and satisfaction than material purchases. All because they are less susceptible to comparison than material purchases. In other words, comparing the digital camera or latest smartphone you bought with your friends during a two week European trip decreases enjoyment over the purchase.

Aknin also found there is positive effect when it comes to fulfilling psychological needs of competence and autonomy. Instead of chasing the next designer good with dead animal skin, why not buy your parents a trip and join in the experience? Generosity is more enjoyable when it is shared as it builds better social connection. In other words, the key to happiness might be spending to share, not to compare. Remember, happiness is priceless.

In the world of business, money is how we transfer wealth. If I do my job right, I create good experiences for my customers, I get paid because society will say, we owe you something in the future for the experience you created in the past, here's a little money.

Professors normally downplay the cutthroat culture of academia, but managers compare business to war which can only be understood if you have skin in the game. Academia never saw that the shifts we are seeing in capitalist exchange over the coming years will reflect a reintegration of sharing economy into a system that has become impersonal and commercial.

As new opportunists capitalize on this new model of capitalism, normal people often sweat our asset and ourselves as hard as we could. Very often, we fail to recognize the full range of possibilities when there is a shift in this new age of capitalism. The internet may not add to the stock of your online listings of properties, but it increases the impact of the audience on your asset that already exists.

Most business schools like to publish business case studies so management consulting firms can give cases to clients to sound smarter during a business presentations. But what is the point of case studies? Will case study be an indicator how good you will be as a consultant? Almost everyday, traditional businesses are getting disrupted by new technologies. Because in reality, it is not about finding the right or wrong answer, bur rather the method you use to generate a profit from business. It is about the strategic moves you make, the issues you identify as you build your business, the frameworks you use, the creativity involved because as entrepreneurs, we are the ones who have skin in the game.

A complete understanding of the frameworks and concepts in the later section is very important to build a successful Airbnb empire. Most hosts plan to have single listing. But in cracking the code of Airbnb equation, you have to have at least one framework and start building multiple listings. Often times, you will be faced with the problem at hand like not responding fast enough to texts, outsourcing cleaners or lost keys. This approach also indicates that creativity or analytical thought on your part can help increase your daily income per listing. The more listings you have, the more comfortable you will become implementing this framework, the more you will start to double of triple your income with your multiple listing of properties.

You are also expected to make sound judgement as to which

automation framework are approve and what are the problems you most commonly faced at hand. Your framework will be the enablers that organize and guide your thinking in automating your business. The combination of your own creativity and preparation are the driving force to your framework. When a freelance fashion stylist, Issie Gibbons first used Airbnb to book a private read in Marrakech five years ago, it changes the way the freelance fashion stylist would travel in the future.

The best way to experience it is by staying in an Airbnb the next time you travel. You would soon realize it is cheaper and you could have the while place to yourself. More importantly, it will change the way you travel in the future. Imagine the same thing happening to millions of travelers around the world.

I still could recall my first Airbnb experience in picturesque Queenstown, New Zealand where I collected keys of my rental car from the airport and drove to my Airbnb townhouse where the mountains were covered in powdered snow. I prefer the quirkiness and originality of Airbnb where I could just go the local grocery store and cook myself dinner during a cold winter evening. I've always hated the impersonal feel of most hotels, the boutique ones are fine, but Airbnb is so much cheaper, so I always go to there first.

Even hotel operators in the Dunstane hotel in Edinburg noticed changes in booking pattern over the past couple of years. The commercial manager said "We find that Airbnb is filling up first and it's taking longer for guys to fill key dates, such as the festival. It's the same on weekends- Saturday nights are slower. She added "It's harder work now, so we've looked at widening our channels to make ourselves more competitive and the hotel has turned to luxury travel agents to increase its visitor numbers. On the plus side, Airbnb has done a lot in terms of exposing millennials to travel and is forcing everyone especially the hotel industry to up their game.

With the privilege of getting to work with many entrepreneurs throughout my career, I can square the consumerist ethic with capitalist of a business person. The difference of that the rich take great care in managing their assets and investments and the less well heeled often go into debt buying cars or the newest television they don't really need.

During my college days, I lived frugally, minding every penny saved up to test various businesses which mostly failed. Because running out of money means I don't have to worry about what to buy. When I was in my younger days, I was insanely tracked and insanely competitive. But you tend to miss out on a lot of other things in life, you tend to miss important family gatherings, you tend to skip social gatherings, your intimate partner might leave you because you are always working. This was too tough for most, because modern day consumerism has taught us to indulge what is good for you. And being frugal is oppression.

Travel has taken a whole new form in the 21st century. London is not a city or Japan a country, there are all experiences to broaden our horizon to make us happier. Working corporate people normally tell their friends to 'follow you heart' or to just place that down payment on that brand new fancy car so you could work an extra 15 hours per week and perhaps go travel in a distant land so you can escape from work life. In a consumerism world, most people go though life "in pursuit of life and in pursuit of pleasure".

The mind is a flow of subjective experiences, such as pain, pleasure anger and love. Emotions and though which flash for a brief moment and immediately disappear. There are experiences can flicker and vanish in a moment so having more experiences through traveling gives people reflect on stand we often try to sort the experiences into buckets of experience such as sensations, euphoria, bliss etc. By scrolling through your *Instagram* feed, it constitutes the flow of subjective experiences of sensation and desire. Because the human minds constantly changes and the conscious experience will always have feeling and wanting new experiences.

The rise of the internet and the improvement in most cities infrastructure brought about new opportunities for the new breed of entrepreneurs. The internet created jobs never heard before, not just for Search Engine Optimization professionals, social media influencers, but also for internet giants like Amazon and Google. It's one thing to consume free information or entertainment, a very different thing to create content which might reach a very large potential audience.

In order to understand the limitations of brick and mortar businesses, imagine that you own a barber shop Brooklyn, New York catering to busy working people. You work so hard in your shop that your scissors become dull. So you harness up hairdressing tools and head to the market town down to give a hair cut for a busy rich banker who wants a haircut in his office and is willing a pay a premium for it. You head down to the banker's office with your professional grade scissor, clipper, straight razor work and styling for his texture of hair.

The banker was very happy with your service and recommended you to his other rich banker friends. Soon enough, you are getting tonnes of requests from hedge fund managers, bankers, high frequency traders and even crypto bros. They are willing to pay a premium for on site haircut in their offices during lunch hour but you can't be going to ten different spots in one time taking ten appointments at one time.

How much should you charge him for the convenience? Every day you encounter dozens of customers in your barbershop but at the same time the market is telling you that there is a base of clients with propensity to pay premium prices. But come to think of it, what the new rich would be doing will be identifying leverage for this business model, since it is somewhat validated by real customers, raise capital, and leverage on the tech side of the business.

Just like a modern day Columbus who pitched the Queen Isabella to finance his journey, this barber created a platform where any upscale barber can register on site, so he now has a website or an app, in exchange for a small fee per successful hair cut. The barber then pitched Venture Capitalists to raise funding for his conquest to dominate this niche. The best way to get back their money, the barber told her, was to make the large corporations pay a much higher price in the near future by providing a share of the company.

In the innovation economy, every day the barber will have to learn anew the relative prices of dozens of clients. If haircuts were performed with one hundred clients, then the barber will have to know the consumer surplus and producer surplus, how do you figure that out?

True, the barber could look for a venture capitalist to invest in his new startup with a traction of say 50 barbers on his platform, called maybe BUBER in New York City serving on site premium priced haircuts with 4,100 different hair cuts, beard trim or hot towel shave. Everyone would work according to their abilities, and received orders according to their ratings which turns out in practice into everyone would work as hard as possible to receive as much as they could grab

Yet this barber found a more easy way to use this platform to connect large number of barbers to high income professionals in New York City. Is he working as hard as other barbers? You bet he is, but he makes money every time a haircut is booked on his platform. The secret is that instead of working 100 hours on his barber catering to maybe 10 clients per day, he could now process 100 clients per day or maybe 10,000 clients per day by scaling his platform to other major cities.

Leverage in business is what the new capitalists are willing to use in order to scale quickly when a business model is proven to work with a small base of clients. Leverage enables people to grow their businesses, tech or non-tech, quickly and easily to offer the product or service to an even wider base of consumers.

The first is to understand leverage and then most people have two choices. The question you should be asking is are you making mistakes of ambition or mistakes of sloth?

The first is the results of a deacon to act, to do something. Of course you will have incomplete information but don't let fear stop you, because we have to accept the fact that in business, it is impossible to have all the facts beforehand. By the time you have all the facts, all other competitors will be jumping into the pool and you don't want to find yourself struggling in a red ocean.

The next is decision of sloth, which is not to do something. If we refuse to change a bad situation out of fear despite having all the facts, you don't take any chances, how can can learn from your experiences? Your bad experience will make you smarter to not repeat it. So before you test your assumptions, remember Fortune favors the Bold.

CHAPTER VI: DIFFERENCE BETWEEN MONEY, WEALTH AND STATUS

Wealth is assets that earn money while you are asleep. Wealth is also money in the bank that is invested into other assets like a stock or into other businesses. Throughout history, money has been used to facilitate trust between both sides in a transaction.

Even property can be a form of wealth, because you can rent that extra room in your house on platforms like Airbnb. Wealth could also be a a portfolio of assets you built that is running at night while serving hundreds of customers.

So the definition of wealth can take many different forms for many people. For me, it's much about building businesses and assets that can earn while you sleep.

There is no company in this world that owns the entire marketplace and every firm in a competitive market not differentiated and most companies sells the same related products. Too often, you see a hot market, and many firms start entering the market, increase supply, drive prices down and destroy profits which was what attracted them in the first place.

If competition gets too intense where too many firms enters a market with razor thin profit margins, some will suffer losses, some will close up shop and then prices will eventually go back to normal. In this new age, that is a very red ocean where you do not want to find yourself in.

Look around at other competitors in your market and see what they are selling. Where do you fit in the ecosystem? Since no firm has absolute market power, we must determine a price where the market demands. The smart people look around a figured out what they could create to escape competition instead of competing head on with big corporations with deep pockets.

The reason you want to identify leverage in this new age is what I mean when I say carving out your own spot in the marketplace to build wealth in this permission less economy. The entire world wants wealth and the entire world is working hard to get it. When you are trading time for money, your income will always be limited. Most of us take seven hours to sleep, about two hours to commute to and from work and another four hours to cook, eat, spending time with family. Hopefully, if we worked hard and long enough, we will save enough money to retire at the age of sixty five.

CHAPTER VII: WHY THE MONEY IN YOUR BANK ACCOUNT IS LOSING VALUE

People also think that government steal money from people. Well, governments don't have to, they just need to print more of it. But you might say, it is much safer to save up and have money in the bank. Nobody needed to invest for the future and I don't want any invisible or visible hands to touch my money.

During the 2008 global recession, the U.S federal government implemented strategies to lower interest rates and quantitative easing (means printing more money), that resulted in a dramatic drop in the value of the dollar. The fact is, by holding your wealth in cash, it is actually eroding. Say you had $100,000 cash saved in your bank account since year 2000, in 2019 the value is only around $51,000. Why? Because your $100,000 can only purchase a basket of goods that is much more expensive today, called inflation. In other words, 51% of the value of your money has evaporated based on the average annual inflation of 3.36%.

If printing money created wealth, there'd be no poverty left on earth.

In certain countries, political parties and groups despise wealth creation. Reducing the game to zero-sum game of status, dragging everybody down to their level. No one pretended that misfortune didn't exits, but prior generations believed in making their own luck by working hard.

But perhaps we've become too quick to dismiss what ethical wealth creation is. We are not talking about monopolies or crony capitalism. We are talking about misplaced externalities like the environment, about free minds and free markets.

In an ecosystem, including our own body, you need a lot of symbiotes, and our cells needs mitochondria to deliver oxygen to our blood for example. If the human body get filled with too much parasites like worms, virus or bacteria and there are purely parasitical, you can die from it. Is there a way for entrepreneurs to succeed in ecosystems with mispriced externalities? Unfortunately not, because companies are not experiments.

In any kind of wealth creation, if a society disrespects these fundamental laws or like Rottenberg experienced in Mexico "Big fishes eating up all the little fishes", then the society will descend into darkness and despair.

Bankers don't need to have skin in the game while still get fat bonuses after causing the subprime mortgage crisis back in 2008. Bernie Madoff designed the largest Ponzi scheme in history and stole $65 billion from his clients. In this world, there's a lot of theft going on all the time, more so in third world countries.

The purpose of wealth for the new rich is freedom, nothing more than that. Not to buy some fancy watch or car, or buy a yacht or jet around in a GulfStream with supermodels. The mistake people make today is they start looking for new opportunities, find one that looks good and start building from there. The problem is, in most competitive markets, the equilibrium were producer supply meets consumer demand normally creates one or two "Perfect Competitors".

The lesson is clear: If you want to create a sustainable business and capture value, don't build the same commoditized product like other businesses.

In this new age of permission less economy, you're not going to get value unless you really want it. To some extent, there are competitive elements to getting wealth because there's a finite amount of reserves to go around in society. If you already have a company, you can us this Airbnb Equation will quickly grow your company and get customers for free. I was hesitant to title this book "The Airbnb Equation", because I didn't want people to dismiss it simply because they sell other non-tech based products besides a purely information based product.

Capitalism fundamental characteristics, private ownership, economic self-self-interest and a marketplace that responds to supply and demand. Many cultures has vowed poverty as an inescapable part of this imperfect world. Social poverty will always be around but in modern society, in most countries, nobody is starving to death. In developed countries, more people are dying from obesity than starvation.

In fact, obesity is now killing triple the number of people than people who die from malnutrition. As many as three million deaths a year is linked to obesity. Free market capitalism is innate to humans and for those reasons, humans can cooperate even if my tech developer is Serbian, my other worker is Chinese or Indian by origin, we can still work together towards a common goal.

If you treat the future to take a definite form, it makes sense to understand it in advance and potentially build a business that is adapting to todays consumers needs. But as you think it the future is dark and uncertain, like Uber displacing cab drivers or Airbnb disrupting the hotel industry, you won't even attempt to work towards mastering it.

Time is your most valuable asset and it is not renewable. It's odd to spend time with working with people who don't have the same long term vision as you. If you can't count on them for a lasting relationships, maybe you haven't invested enough time to build a tightly knit group instead of a transactional relationship. So why work with a group of people who don't even like each other?

CHAPTER IX: IT'S A WINNER TAKE ALL GAME IN THE INNOVATION ECONOMY

The highest prize in Youtube world is unambiguous: out of tens of thousands of full-time *Youtubers* each year, only a few dozen get to make more than a million dollars.

After graduating with a bachelor's degree, I was invited to interview for stock broker with an Investment Bank. My exam to get a Series 7, also called the General Securities Representative Exam went well. I was so close to getting my Series 7 license in the last examination at the SEC. If only I got this brokerage license, I thought, I would be set for life. But I didn't. At that time, I was devastated.

In 2015, after I had built and sold several businesses, I ran into an old pal from the investment bank who had helped me prepare my failed Securities Representative applications. We hadn't spoken for almost a decade and his first question wasn't "How are you?" Or " Wow, it's been such a long time". Instead, he grinned and asked : " So Terrence, aren't you glad you didn't get that representative license?"

With hindsight, we both know that winning that ultimate competition would have changed my life for the worst. I could have passed that exam and I probably would have spent my entire career taking calls or drafting other people's business deals instead of creating anything new. Looking back, it's hard to say how much would be different but the opportunity cost for not working on something I'm passionate about were too great. The logic of my career path was easy to see, I wanted to give to the things that I was most interested in and to the places where I thought I could have the most impact.

To fully appreciate the choice of not choosing the path well worn, or back in late 2000s, you need to know one thing about the brokerage industry, it was moving online and major brokers were offering ultra-low commission fee to eliminate middle men like us. Back in the days, I gave a huge spectrum of issues that seem unrelated at first glance. Fast forward ten years, you can now trade stocks for free by downloading an app like Robinhood.

In modern society, we are trained to have an obsession with competition. Grades are an analytical and very surgical way to know student's performance. Students with the highest grades and credentials receive status and recognition. Students who don't will be left out sitting at the corner to feel inferior. Students compete to higher levels to compete their dreams out of them. Parents pay hundreds of thousands of dollars to have kids compete in a place where competition is so intense so that equally smart classmates can get the same conventional careers like management consulting or investment banking. Are we turning a generation of young people into conformists?

In my early days after a conventionally successful undergraduate career, I wish I had asked myself, why am I competing for the standard badges of success. Winning is always better than losing. But it's always better to know firsthand if the war is worth fighting in the first place. If you can't beat a competition, it's always better to merge.

CHAPTER VIII: THE UBER EQUATION

Before we ask who are your competitors, we have to ask you a personal question. Are you crazily passionate about building an automated cash flow business? Sometimes you do have to fight. It's either all in, strike hard and end it quickly or don't start at all. There is no middle ground. Sometimes people are willing to spend money to compete, but they aren't able. Other corporations have all the money in the world and they are able but not willing to fight this battle.

Airbnb has gained dominance because of network effects and there is little value if you were to go out and start the number one hundredth Airbnb. In the early years of Airbnb, you can't say that for some of the hotel alternatives exist in the city. In fact, probably none. Number two, you have control over the pricing of your listing on Airbnb only takes 3 percent which covers the cost of processing payments. Meaning you keep the 97 percent of pricing in which you fully control. Like Uber implement dynamic pricing, or surge pricing, you can increase the price of your listing when it comes to holiday or peak seasons. When prices go up, you get more profits and when more property owners list their properties on Airbnb, more visitors tend to visit the site. That means less people are stranded and more people have an option to accommodation in their travels.

While companies like Uber take 25 percent per ride, Uber was addressing the chronic shortage of cars during spikes in demands by tailoring the service to people who could afford to pay extra. As an entrepreneur, you should be thinking in terms of consumer surpluses, the kind of economics at play, and visitors would continue to have acceptance to the idea that the same room could cost more at different hotels in the same vicinity.

When there is an outlast at Uber's CEO Travis Kalanick about implementing surge pricing, riders would continue to have visceral resistance to the idea that the same ride could cost more at different times. But Kalanick's stubborn defense seems to impress another true entrepreneur, Amazon CEO Jeff Bezos. Bezos told board member Bill Gurley after the surge pricing implementation that "Travis is a real entrepreneur." He added "Most CEOs would have caved."

I have hundreds of stories of new rich I could tell you about. People who have taken their talents, ideas, and unique abilities and make millions from it in this permission less economy. One of my favorite story is Joe Rogan.

In certain developing countries where crony capitalism can also result in monopoly since they want their monopoly profits to be unmolested. Crony capitalism can spill over the government, political and the media. Ecosystems in emerging markets is important is encourage startups. Linda Rottenberg who founded an entrepreneur accelerator visited Mexico for the first time.

What she never imagined was, she was sitting in a room with the most affluent Mexicans in the country, names like Emilio Azcárraga Jean and Lorenzo Zambrano. Linda wanted to know why the entrepreneurship ecosystem doesn't grow like other parts of Latin American. Their answer , "because in Mexico, the big fish eat the little fish."

Our fortune, in the next decades will be intricately connected to our community structure and with the internet, this can be made possible.

WEALTH IS A POSITIVE SUM GAME

Wealth is a very positive sum game in the innovation economy. Everyone can own a property in this world, because you own a property, it doesn't mean it takes away my ability to own a property. The more we know about building properties, the more people that can have properties.

In essence, there are two fundamental games people play in life. One is the money game. Another is status game. People realize that money is not going to solve all problems, but lack of it can solve no problems. The lack-of money highway is a sure path to misery. I think people realize that so they want to make money.

Meanwhile, people are stuck thinking that they can't make it and they don't want to create any wealth because they don't believe it can happen. So it's easy to frame money and attack the whole system by saying "Money is evil and you shouldn't make it".

Status on the other hand is a zero sum game. For someone to win, another will have to lose. This is even more obvious in sports where only one team or person can emerge a winner and the other must be a lower.

On the evolutionary basis, even the animal kingdom struggle for survival, aggression and battle. In 1970, Richard Ryder while campaigning in Oxford denote a ubiquitous type of human centered prejudice. Racism violates the principle of equality.

It is how we conceptualize ourselves and our world but that is no more interesting than being born in Malaysia or Canada. Discrimination or prejudice will always be a central tool creating creating human supremacy and exceptionalism. All these things are tied to status. Almost every decision you've ever made was based on this one subconscious question.

Discrimination based on race, is thought to be prejudicial because there are not characteristics that matter when it comes to making moral claims. Thus, if you go back thousands of years, status if much better predictor of survival than wealth is.

Hunter-gatherers thousands of years ago couldn't store wealth before the agricultural age. So hunter-gatherers had to carry everything on their backs and this created status based societies. Even in modern societies, the status game can also be skewed towards wealth-based societies.

By attacking the rich, journalists can have the most substantive advantage because they are saying to the rich: "No, my audience is much more important and therefore me as a journalist, I represent the people, therefore I am more important."

To win the status game, you have to put someone else down. As a good rule of thumb in building your wealth, you would always avoid playing status games because you could become an angry and always picking fights. Most of your time will be spent putting everyone else down to put yourself or the people you like up on the pedestal.

THE STATUS GAME IS A ZERO SUM GAME

The clearest way to not play the status game is to realize it early on. Status games are inevitable and they will always exist because when you are trying to create wealth, bigger corporations will be attacking you to make them appear higher status. Whether it is attempting to increase their status at your expense, they are playing a different game and it's a zero sum game, not a positive sum game.

You can choose to play a zero sum status game, or you can choose to radically improve and existing solution that would certainly support a cash flow business.

If you focus a lot on business near-term growth, be it a business or growing an audience, you might miss the most important question, "Will this business be around in ten years from now?" Vanity metrics such as number of likes or followers doesn't pay the bills. Numbers alone won't tell you the full picture. A more critical question will be what are the qualitative characteristics of your business.

ARE WE REALLY LIVING IN A POST SCARCITY WORLD?

There's a notion you probably heard "money is the root of all evil." In fact, my high school English teacher gave us this little title to write an essay on but I was only 16 at the time. Little did I know how complex the world is. I probably scored an F for that paper. So I'm writing this book to hopefully have a better reflection of reality after years of getting my face smashed to the pavement of Wall Street and cut-throat business world.

People think that bankers steal money from hardworking people. Well, it's somewhat true. Bankers don't need to have skin in the game while still get fat bonuses after causing the subprime mortgage crisis back in 2008. Bernie Madoff designed the largest Ponzi scheme in history and stole $65 billion from his clients. In this world, there's a lot of theft going on all the time, more so in third world countries.

When Forbes interviewed Elon Musk, a serial South African born entrepreneur who co-founded PayPal, later Tesla and SpaceX, : "Do you ever wish you had lived during a different time in history?"

Musk replied;" No, I'm glad I'm alive now." He then added " If anyone thinks they'd rather be in a different part of history, they're probably not a very good student of history. Life sucked in the old days. People knew very little, and you were likely die at a young age of some horrible disease. You'd probably have no teeth by now."

Good point. The evolution of the internet has created an unlimited wealth machine. Disruption is not just a buzzword but corporations like Blockbuster once told Reed Hastings of Netflix to go away when Hastings wanted Blockbuster to buy Netflix for $50 Million. Netflix is now worth $129 Billion and Blockbuster filed for chapter 11 in 2010.

In the past decades, gatekeepers of capitalism, emerged as the preferred venue to introduce (or reintroduce) yourself to the world. The large majority of creative work did not get to see the light of the day. In this new age, failure is an acceptable option. There's hardly anyone this book who hasn't tasted it.

Today entrepreneurship capitalism has created instant celebrities and how they achieved they quick wins. In this book, we show how you can identify the underlying drivers that have help accelerate the new model of entrepreneurship. Every industry is now in the technology space, whether it is food, hotels, music or transportation. There is an app for everything you can think of, and thus ripe for pillaging.

What if you can rewind to 2004 and create 1,000 copies of Facebook and in each copy see how many times it would succeed? Reality is much more complicated but referencing what reporter Alexis Madrigal in The Atlantic said in his tweet " Success is never accidental."

Let's take a brief look at success from the Renaissance and the Industrial revolution in the mid-20th century. Can we create luck? Is luck something to be mastered, dominated or even controlled? Ralph Waldo Emerson beautifully illustrates luck: " Shallow men believe in luck, believe in circumstances… Strong men believe in cause and effect."

In this book, you will discover how victory awaits the person who has everything in order-luck, people call it. Prior generation believed making their own luck by working hard, but if you believe that creating a successful business all depends on luck, why read this book? Did Mark Zuckerberg simply win the social media lottery or was Elon Musk born with a silver spoon, or did he wait for luck to happen for *Tesla, SpaceX & the Boring Company*?

While I'm not telling you to read about other startup founders biography because when we put luck into the equation, we are not learning anything about building your next potential breakthrough business. The right question should be what business models with leverage should I be choosing? With luck in the past tense, the next question should be how does the fastest growing companies take advantage of the present scale economies, is it a matter of chance or design?

A lot of young entrepreneurs today want to do everything, because everyone around them has long since lost faith in a definite world. Instead of working tirelessly on one project, young people today want to pursue ten different things. People lack concrete plans to carry out a project. In a permission less economy with endless choices, the one best thing to do is to have firm conviction on one thing and be really good at it. In other words, a monopoly of one.

Young people are fascinated by the great fortunes being made by startup founders, YouTubers, Instagram Influencers, but they pay less attention to the process successful New Rich trying hard to get a viable base of audience. Millennials are definite optimists, they are taught that the future will be better than the present is he plans and works to make it better.

Yes, money is important but it doesn't solve all your problems. The first thing you realize is that after making a bunch of money is that you're still the same person. I know lots of rich people who are out of shape and deeply unhappy. Jeff Bezos still has to work out like the rest of us even if he has all the money in the world. But to have a fit body, a calm mind and meaningful relationships requires work and there is no shortcut to it.

To me the ultimate purpose of money is that you don't have to be in a specific place, a specific time doing the thing you hate to do. Money is less about buying dumb shit in the material world, rather it's giving you the freedom to not do the things you don't want to do.

Each generation is defined by it's inventions and visionaries. After a brief pessimistic phase in the late 2000s, indefinite optimism has dominated millennial thinking, when a long bull market from 2009 to todays writing 2019 began and tech companies eclipsed traditional companies as the way to approach the future. But, he doesn't know exactly how to approach the future, so he won't make any specific plans. He expects to profit from the future but sees no reason design a concrete plan and execute it relentlessly.

Whether you were born in 1985, 1990 or even 2000, things for better every years for the first 18 years of your life and it had nothing to do with you. Then, when the internet moved from desktops to handheld devices, every year of adulthood tends to get a little better and better for the middle class. Forbes magazine and Fast Companies are filled with millennials but the rest of their generation was getting left behind, but the rest of millennials fail to question their naive optimism.

Since entrepreneurship has become sexy compared to their parents generation, when Baby Boomers were making more than the average millennial today, Millennials grew up so used to effortless progress that they feel entitled to it.

When a millennial grows up and write books to explain why other millennials are successful, they point to the power of a particular individual's contact as determined by luck. But this is not why this book is written, in fact we will be making a contrarian critique of the myth of the self-made entrepreneurs in a permissionless economy.

Today's parents don't expect their kids to become astronauts any more than they expect them to become an Instagram Influencer. From an early age, we are all taught to take things step by step and day by day or improve our scores grade by grade. But the audience today seems to be more accessible than ever.

The second most common reason stopping people from starting a cash flow business is risk aversion. What if I start that business and they turn out to be not working? If you goal is to not make a mistake then you shouldn't be looking for the next business opportunity or leverage. The idea of being lonely but right is already hard, commitment into something you believe will work. But the idea of being lonely and wrong, to most, is very painful.

Next is complacency. Most social elites has the freedom and ability to pursue things that interest them. For instance, family offices managing wealth from previous generations may not build and run a startup. Why search for a new startup idea when you can comfortably collect rents from the businesses you have in your portfolio? In most Ivy Leagues orientation days, incoming class are being told if you get into this prestigious institution, all your worries should go away and you will be set for life.

Finally, people might think if there is an undiscovered idea, wouldn't someone from this faceless world discovered it already? There are millions of smarter and more creative people that will have found it and this can discourage people from starting anything. While you were shuffling your fantasy roster, there are a few other ideas in todays permissionless economy I want to go through.

THE PRINCIPAL-AGENT PROBLEM

The principal-agent problem. To distinguish a principal and an agent, who the principal is an owner. Agent works for the principal so in a business setting, you can think of an agent as an employee. And there is a difference of thinking between a principal and an agent.

Benjamin Franklin wrote in the Poor Richard's Almanack : "If you would have your business done, go: if not send." And "If you were a servant would you not be ashamed that a good master should catch you idle? Then if you are your own master be ashamed to catch yourself idle."

In a nutshell, a principal's incentives are different than an agent's incentives. In the Airbnb equation, most the operations can be outsourced which includes, key handling, cleaning services and even message handling so you don't get texts 3 am in the morning by your tenant asking how to turn the heater on.

What if I have a full time job? Then your most important job to build a system around your portfolio of properties and to think like a principal. What would you do if you were the owner? There's an optimistic way to describe the result when you think like a principal, because you are setting yourself up to become a principal. Every good principal will promote you when they have faith that you are an accountable person which is a form of leverage.

The key is to understand that principal and agents are highly separated and this can be true even in big companies. You might think that working with the big four in management consulting will give you better results. Yes, they might have more people and an established brand, but very often, there is still a separation of principal and agent because the work done by agents who simply doesn't care as much.

How must you see the world if you know there is a separation of principal and agent? You'd have to believe that the work done by an agent will have varied results. On the contrary, by building your portfolio of properties that generate cash flow every week, you are betting big on that person to get the job done because his or her accountability is on the line, in most cases, their job is just to change the sheets and place fresh towels and a piece of wrapped soap on the bed.

Other people can be one of our greatest sources of happiness, but sometimes it can be a distraction. Since creation is normally embarrassing and the creative process can sometimes be inhibited by others, when you have a new great idea, there are normally thousands of other stupid ones. Sara Blakely of *Spanx* said that "Ideas are fragile in their infancy."

So should you tell everyone if you have an unconventional idea like leasing a hut in Bali and converting it into a listing for $500 per night? There is a sweet spot between telling nobody and telling everybody and that's where a cash cow is created. More often than not, a great listing idea is built around a secret that is not outwardly displayed on the front end.

Sometimes alone time can be important for creation and this state of mind got her Minimum Viable Product out into the world instead of seeking validation from the closest people she knew. Most million-dollar are squashed because people want to tell you their concerns.

Studies have found that just fifteen minutes of solitude without electronic devices can actually have positive effects such as decreased anxiety, less lonely or sad. Alone time accentuates low-key emotions, while dialing down what we really value.

Accountability is a simple concept, to take on accountability. Where every member take on accountability where every team member take on

Specific knowledge is often highly technical or creative. It cannot be outsourced or automated.
Embrace accountability, and take business risks under your own name. The marketplace will reward you with cash flow, good reviews, and leverage.

Labor means people working for you. It's the oldest and most sought-over form of leverage. Labor leverage will impress your parents, but don't waste your life chasing it. Apply specific strategy, with leverage, and eventually you will get what you deserve. When you're finally wealthy, you'll realize that it wasn't what you were seeking in the first place. But that's for another day.

Apply specific knowledge, with leverage, and eventually you will get what you deserve. Whether you are an interior designer, freelancer, Fortune 500 company executive, you can start building your virtual empire with very little capital.

Show them the prior listings, Work as hard as you can. Even though who you work with and what you work on are more important than how hard you work.

Leverage is a force multiplier for your judgement.

Technology will help increase our mastery and reduce the role of chance in our lives. Building a business in a permission less economy could actually bring scale back with a vengeance.

But even if succeeding in todays permission less economy is a real possibility rather than an imponderable mystery, it will happen to your business it you understand the levers. Indefinite fears about the future shouldn't stop us from making definite plans today. For the few who understands how to navigate this economy, there is room in between for new age of entrepreneurs to build a vastly better business that can scale. As we apply this specific knowledge to create wealth, they won't just get better at all aspects of things you already do, they will help to do what was previously unimaginable.

You can't find leverage without looking for them. If you think that something is hard and impossible, you will never even start trying to achieve it. Belief in using leverage in todays scale economies is an effective truth. One day, we could cure cancer, dementia and generate energy without using fossil fuels. However, we will never learn to look into places that give us leverage to makes those possible if you don't force ourselves to look hard.

Before Uber, passenger had little choice but to pay high prices for taxi services. Passengers couldn't easily and reliably get a ride but Uber san the untapped supply and unaddressed demand where other saw nothing at all.

It all started when the founders couldn't get a cab in Paris and started seeing that we already had a GPS device in our pockets why not use that to connect drivers and passengers? More often than not, Internet companies underestimated the power of simplicity, in itself could be a starting point of building an important and valuable business. Yes, you can start looking for ideas where no body is looking.

Airbnb is a true marketplace and it's worth doing some research on active listings around you, you can see pricing, photos, headlines or description that make up a successful listing in your market. The best way to to use Airbnb's data-driven powerful search functionality.

Before building your portfolio of Airbnb properties, you will need to ask yourself. How will the constant addition of new places affect my ability to consistently get reservations at the best possible rates?

Let's say you have a 2-bedroom, 1 bathroom apartment in Singapore Central Business District. You offer the entire place, two beds, WIFI and a kitchen. The first step is to identify your direct Airbnb competition. For example, from Airbnb's initial Singapore search page, you can filter your selections by the dimensions seen below.

1.) USING AIRBNB'S SEARCH FILTERS TO RESEARCH YOUR COMPETITION

Using these filters, Airbnb lists 300+ rentals in this area. You know that the central business district is a large neighborhood, and parts are more popular (which is relevant to many cities throughout the world). You can then narrow down using the map to zoom in and the results will refresh, narrowing you down to 110+ listings

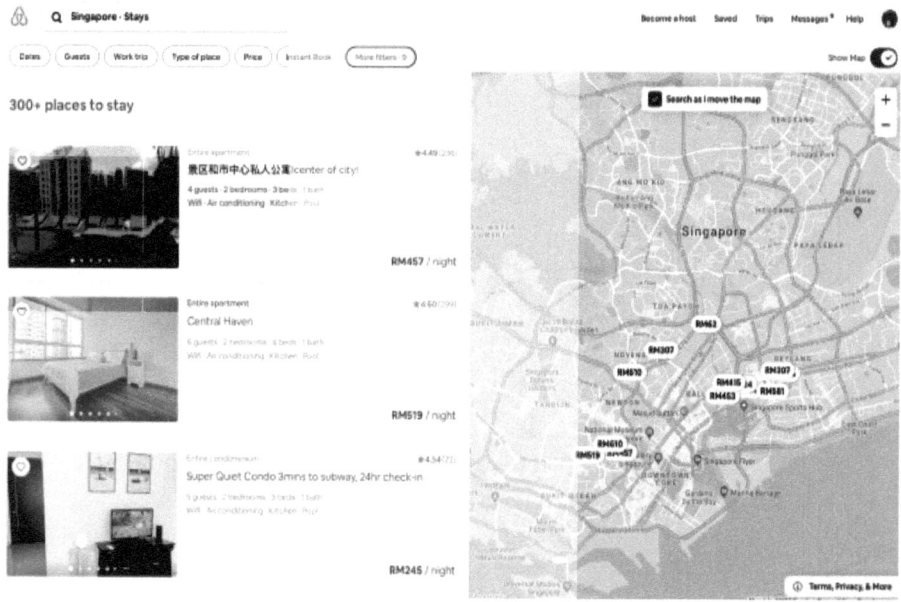

THE AIRBNB EQUATION

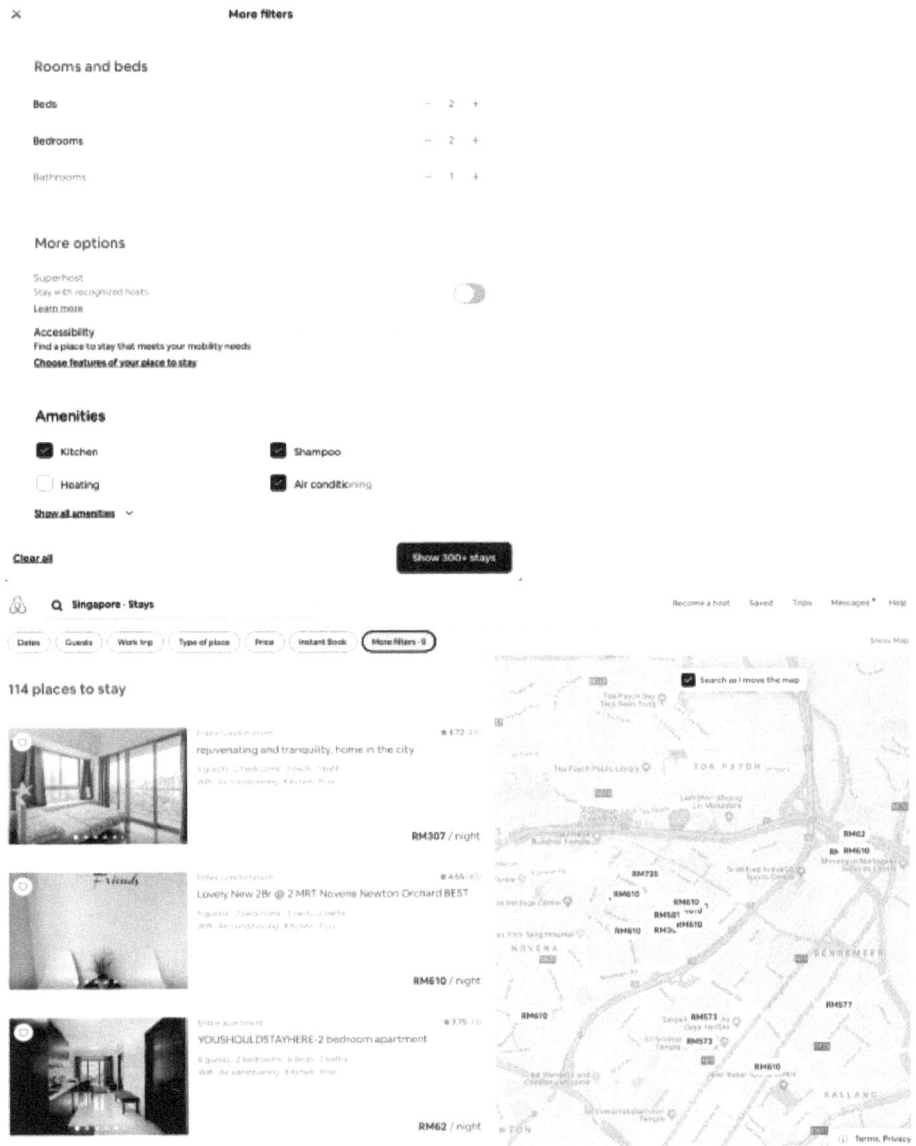

2.) COMPILE THE RESULTS INTO A SPREADSHEET

Next, is to build a list of similar listings and compile them into a spreadsheet for analysis. You can also use web data extraction tools to save you hours of work. Once you have downloaded all the info into a spreadsheet, narrow down the results with number of reviews you have on your listing with the following metrics:

- Average number of reviews, 5-20 reviews
- Average nightly rate

3.) ANALYZE YOUR COMPETITION AND START BUILDING YOUR LIST OF AIRBNB PROPERTIES

Analyzing your competition on a regular basis can give you a clearer picture what might affect future performance of your listing. Cash offers pure optionality and number of your listing still tied to one and only one thing. The success of your listing. If one of your listing fail to over the monthly, all you risk is that one or two months deposit held by the landlord.

All human are pessimists because we have descended from a few thousand years ago to avoid the saber tooth tigers. Human's priority is not get eaten and we're hardwired to be pessimists. In modern society especially the business world, there are no saber tooth wandering around and it is very unlikely you will get eaten by a tiger.

In modern day society, the upside is often unlimited with downside limited. But we only react negatively to potential risks in business. If you don't know any potential upside, it's not because you haven't encountered them, bur rather because upside risk is hidden in plain sight. So adapting for modern society requires overriding your pessimism, taking calculated risk and optimistic bets because the upside is unlimited. People who do that might start the next Tesla, Uber or Amazon, raking in billions of dollars for the society, and creating tremendous wealth for yourself and changing the world.

But what if you fail? You probably lose a few hundred bucks of initial deposit, which you expect to be part of the statistic because you've got another listings generating a cash flow and you can take chances on new properties that will position you to generate future positive cash flows.

The optimist's grail is looking for economic opportunities which is aligned to his or her interest. Thus, the most fundamental requirement to create wealth for yourself in modern society is to be optimistic today, especially if you're educated and living in developing countries where opportunities are boundless.

Even though, some illegal businesses can be highly lucrative, it is not worth the risk of ruin. Risk of ruin means you can be going to jail for a long time and wear an orange jumpsuit. So don't commit any offenses that might put you in these type of risk and this might mean staying out of physically dangerous activities. There is a saying the fatality rate per unit distance on a motorcycle is 35 times greater than an automobile, and third world commercial airline is 35 times safer than an automobile while a first world commercial airline is 35 times safer than a third world commercial airline. In pure statistical terms, deadly events can be catastrophic.

It is also true when building your Airbnb portfolio to not lose all capital and savings on one bet. Take rationally optimistic bets with a huge upside. Most businesses lifeline is advertising, marketing and sales. When you list on Airbnb, they take care of all that. In traditional businesses or the real estate brokerage industry, it takes capital to advertise to drive more business to your company. The most fundamental reason that even founders underestimate the importance of sales is the systematic effort to sell themselves at every level of every field in the business world.

The fundamental path to create a sustainable growth trajectory and the future path of your business are results of persuasion.

There will be people who will try to build up your ideas and build on your ideas. So it's better to think about designing an effective distribution strategy that is part of the design of your product.

If you invented a good product but if you have no effective way to sell it, you've got a bad business. If you have one distribution channel to getting consistent customers after trying a few channels, you have a good business. But If you spread yourself too thinly across few distribution channels and don't nail one, your business will be toast.

Capital is a powerful form of leverage, it is very surgical, it is very analytical.

If you are a great investor and were given a billion dollars and you can make a 30% returns with it and everybody else can only make 20% return, you're going to get all the money and be paid very handsomely for it. Thus, if you get good at managing capital you can manage more and more capital much more easily. The truth is, it is much more easier to manage more capital than people so is a good form of leverage.

Capital & Investment flow into countries with stable money like the US dollar. Stable currency is the foundation of prosperity. Capital gave birth to innovations like the steam engine, railroads and the industrial revolution.

The hard part of capital is how you obtain it and that's why I talked about specific knowledge and accountability. First, if you have specific knowledge in a domain and if you're accountable and you have a good name in that domain, people are going to give you capital.

Once you get capital as a form of leverage, you can use that to go get more capital and this is fairly well understood. The innovation of capital is the most interesting in todays digital economy because it is the idea of products having no marginal cost of replication.

THE THREE TYPES OF LEVERAGE IN WEALTH CREATION

1.) Labor as a Form of Leverage

Everybody understands labor as a form of leverage, the society overvalues labor as a form of leverage. This is why your parents are impressed when you get a promotion and lots of people working underneath you. This is why a lot of NAIVE people ask you when you have a company and how many people work there, and they used that as a way to establish credibility to measure how much leverage you have. As Artificial Intelligence is going to replace normal repetitive work, renting out your time will not be getting you rich. In fact, it might make repetitive work obsolete.

But I would argue this is the worst form of leverage you can possibly have in the permission less economy. Managing other people is incredibly messy. It requires tremendous leadership skills. You are one step away from getting fired with a wrong decision, or getting torn by the mob.

It is incredibly competed over, just check your last Online Job Application Tab and see how many applied for the same job you did, entire civilization has been destroyed over this fight. For example, communism or marxism is a battle between capital or labor, so it's a trap.

Bottomline, you want to stay out of labor leverage, you want the minimum amount of people working for you that is going to allow you to use the OTHER FORMS of leverage, which is CAPITAL, this type of leverage is a little more interesting because large amount of capital is being moved around or being saved.

2.) NEW FORM OF LEVERAGE IN THE DIGITAL ECONOMY

This form of leverage has been invented in the last few hundred years when it started with the printing press and then broadcast media and now it's really blown up with the internet. So now you can multiply your efforts without having to involve other humans and without needing money from other humans.

This book self-published on Amazon is a form of leverage. Not too long ago, I would have had to sit in a publishers hall. One in a hundred is not good odds, you may be thinking. Especially for debut authors, the likelihood of getting your manuscript published may seem impossible. Even with publisher's support, the average book sells fewer than 250 copies a year.

But increasingly available with modern technology that both allows for faster production (the literal writing and researching) and wider community support. I can also test the title of this book with A/B split tests before finalizing the title of this book with data sets. I can also do some online research on trending topics in the personal finance or entrepreneurship space before even deciding what topics to dive deep into and start writing.

About thirty years ago, I would have to be lucky to get on TV based on someone else's leverage, they would have just ordered the message and taken the economics out of it or charge me for it so they would have model the message. And I would have to be lucky to get that form of leverage but today thanks to the internet.

I can buy a cheap microphone, hook up to a laptop or iPad and start a podcast so this new form of leverage is where all the new fortunes are made.

In sum, the last generation fortunes were made by capital that were the Warren Buffetts of the world but the new generation fortunes are all made through code or media.

Joe Rogan makes $50 Million per year with just three employees. That means he is making $75,000 per episode for a 30 minutes podcast where an average American household income was $61,372 per year. PewDiePie makes about $9 million from Youtube ads with combined earnings of $124 million, but these are examples of the new rich leveraging on the permission less economy.

Of course Jeff Bezos, Mark Zuckerberg, Larry Page and Sergey Brin are all using code based leverage, the beauty is when you combine all of these three is where you will excel in taking just the minimum input but the highest output labor you can get.

With engineers, product developers and then you have access to capital and use that as a form for marketing, advertising and scaling, this will be the magical combination and that's why you see technology startups explode out of nowhere. Where you apply massive leverage and make outsized returns.

PERMISSIONS VS PROVISIONAL

The new forms of leverage is that it is permission less. They don't require somebody else's permission for you to use my contents or products. In traditional industries, somebody has to decide to follow you and for capital, somebody has to give you money to invest or to turn it into a product.

With code based leverage, you can start writing books, recording podcasts or Youtube videos. These kind of contents are permission less because you don't need anyone's permission to do that and that's why they are egalitarian, and those platforms are the great equalizer of leverage. That said, everyone can be a broadcaster but you might say Apple might have a slightly closed ecosystem like the App Store but everyone's writing apps for the iPhone so long you can write apps for it, you can get rich.

In modern society, people can grab this low overuse and this is why people learn to code and it is because we have this idea that in the future there is going to be these robots.

They're going to be doing everything and that may be true but I would say the majority of the robot revolution has already happened and the robots are already here. There are way more robots than humans it's just that we packed the in data centers for heat efficiency reasons and we put them in service inside of computers.

Much of todays's white collar work is taking in and processing information and then make decision and recommendations based on that information. Which is exactly what Ai algorithms do best. Self autonomous cars will remove the need for a driver but we will need people to build the underlying software. With scale economies, self autonomous vehicles will allow the sale of those vehicles to drop drastically and get better over time.

CHAPTER X: CODE BASED LEVERAGE

Inside the computer and all the circuits, the robot mind inside that's doing all the work and so every great software developer for examples now has an army of robots working for him day and night.

When he or she sleeps after all the coding she has been cranking away, the robots army keeps working. The robot revolution was already here and the robot revolution is probably halfway through. It is just that we are heading in a much more hardware component these days as we get more comfortable with the idea of autonomous vehicle and maybe autonomous trucks. Boston Dynamics robots and all that robots doing web searching for you for example are already here.

The ones cleaning up your video and audio in transmitting it around the world are already here. The ones answering many customer service queries that you would otherwise have to call for are already here. In fact, an army of robots are already here and it's very cheaply available and the bottleneck is just figuring out the intelligent and interesting things to do with them.

To get code based leverage, you can order this army of robots around the commands that has to be issued in a computer language and in the language that they understand. These robots aren't that smart yet and have to be told very precisely what to do and how to do it so coding is such a great superpower because now you can speak the language of the robot armies and you can tell them what to do.

Think of this point where people are not only commanding the army of robots within servers through code and directly manipulating the movement of trucks of other people who just ordered the package on Amazon. You are also manipulating the movement of many people and many robots to get a package delivered to your doorstep.

There's also an army of actual robots and people that are being manipulated to software labor capital which are much less egalitarian not just in the inputs but actual outputs because they need something that humans have to provide. For instance, if I want to have a massage or if I need a chef to cook my food, as these are the more human element providing that service and the less egalitarian it is.

WILL AI DRIVE YOU OUT OF BUSINESS?

In the new world order illustrated by Kai Fu Lee, the transformation into an AI-driven economy will have a major impact at least in one generation. Many of the hardware or productivity-increasing products will be AI products with algorithms and this can be scaled instantly across all platforms easily around the world. For instance, Tesla's vehicle software system will update new features and improvements remotely, which is instantly distributable within all Tesla's vehicles to add new features like improving battery life, making adjustments to adaptive suspension system or even using 'dampening algorithms' to better handle speeds over 100mph or 160kph.

Compared to the innovations in the 20th century like steam power or electricity, for these algorithm to scale rapidly or gain traction, you need a physical product or hardware to be delivered to the end users. The downside of AI algorithms embedded in hardware devices, every time you make marginal improvements to these hardware, it requires the algorithms to be created again causing an overall slow down in deployment of new technologies.

AI algorithms however have zero marginal cost of replication. Digital algorithms can be distributed with no extra cost and once distributed, they can be constantly updated and improved for free. Programmers can roll out these invisible force of code based army quickly which will threaten white collar workers.

China is known for notoriously knocking off products in the West. Copying for most Chinese is a cultural acceptance, scarcity mental and willingness to dive into any promising new industry has created a new generation of young entrepreneurs shaping the foundations of the Chinese Internet ecosystem. Even China's copycat tradition is not just products but entrepreneurs themselves.

A company called *Xiaomi*, launched a low-cost smartphone that exploded in growth. Even its founder has shamelessly copied products like the iPhone, MacBook and Apple Stores sleek minimalist design. The omnipresent advertising campaigns all over China with low price positioning and the lingering nimbus of Steve Job's playful keynote speeches all contribute to the perception that *Xiaomi* offers products so good as to constitute a category of their own.

For example Jeff Bezos probably has a much better vacation than most of us because he has lots of humans running around doing whatever he needs to do but if you look at the output of code and media, the same product that is proven successful to everybody can turn into a positive sum game where Jeff Bezos doesn't get to watch better movies and TV than we do. Jef Bezos doesn't get to even have a better computing experience or search experience, Google doesn't give him some premium exclusive Google account where his searches are better than other people like us.

From a code based standpoint, billionaires like Jeff would consume on his own where is with other products that is not true. If you look at something like buying a Rolex that's a zero-sum game if everybody in the world is wearing a Rolex then people don't want to wear Rolexes anymore because they are no longer a signal when it effect has been effectively cancelled out.

Rich people have an advantage in consuming that product that are priced up and then other people can relax because it's about you. But something like watching Netflix or using Google or Youtube are not going to be better for rich people from a code based standpoint.

Even Modern-day cars, you want to be in a sweet spot like a *Tesla*

Model 3 or a *Honda Civic* which is an amazing car. Rich people don't have better cars they just have weirder cars. You can drive a *Lamborghini* on the street at any speed that makes sense for *Lamborghinis* which is actually a worst car on the street and it just turned into a signaling good. Because it's mainstream, the technology has amortized cost of production over the large number of consumers possible and the best products tend to be at the centre at that sweet spot for the middle class rather than the upper class.

THE EGALITARIANISM OF MODERN DAY GOODS

Most of the goods and services today we consume are becoming much more egalitarian. Even food is becoming cheap and abundant at least in the first world. Jeff Bezos isn't necessarily eating better foot, he is just eating different food of he's eating food that are prepared to serve theatrically so it's almost like more in the human element of performance rather than the labor element of food product.

The capital element of food is going down massively and unit production itself has become more technology-technology-oriented. The gap between the haves and the have nots is getting smaller so if you care about ethics in Wealth Creation it is better to create your wealth using code and media as leverage because those products are equally available to everybody as opposed to trying to create your wealth through labor or capital because what I'm referring to here is scale economies.

Technology products and media products have such an amazing scale economy that you always want to use the product that us used by the most people. And the one that's used by the most people ends up having the largest budget and there's no marginal cost of adding another user.

The best TV shows are actually not going to be some of the unreleased versions just made for a few rich people. There is going to be a big budget for a show like *Game of Thrones* or *House of Cards*, they will have massive leverage with scale by getting to a certain quality level.

Your rich uncle might want to be different because he has to fly to *Sundance* and watch a documentary and that can actually turn into a signaling good to show other people that he is wealthy and he tried to convert them to status as a poster.

Therefore capital is a form of leverage that have a negative externality and coding product have an ever positive externality attached to them. Capital and also cryptocurrencies like *Libra* is also starting to become a little more permission less or at least the permission is diffused because of the internet. Instead of labor we have a community now which is diffused form of labor. For example, Mark Zuckerberg has a billion people doing work for him by using Facebook and instead of going to raise capital from someone who's rich now, we have crowdfunding platforms so you can raise millions and billions of dollars for charity or a health problem or a a business.

You can do it all online so capital and labor are also becoming permission less and you don't need to do the old fashioned away we have to go around and ask people for permission to use their money or other questions like a choice of business model or a choice product.

PRICE DISCRIMINATION

We all know that your $9.99 per month *Spotify* streaming is not going to sound better beyond HD format. The secret when building a business in the permission less economy is that you can still charge people for extras based on their propensity to pay.

Now that we understood the power of zero marginal cost of replication and scale economies, how do we price our products & services effectively?

To understand this, say a business-class seat that usually cost five to ten times more than economy seats. In actuality, it costs the airline maybe two or three times more than a standard seat. But airline understand people value perks like wider seats, more legroom and better service.

The truth is, rich people and large enterprises are willing to pay more. For those reasons, you can charge a premium to give them the extra little things to signal that they're rich and provide that premium or little bit of comfort they want.

HOW TECH COMPANIES GAIN A BIG BASE OF USERS

We have all seen how enterprise software companies like *Dropbox* uses a freemium model to offer a free or very-low price version to achieve scale. But if you want more space or faster uploads or analytics or multiple-user administration, you'll find yourself paying five to ten times more.

Even music streaming services like *Spotify* is using a freemium model, building a base of 207 Million monthly active users and 117 million active paid subscribers as of this writing 2019. But let's dive deeper into how Spotify disrupted the music industry in just less than 10 years.

Not too long ago, if you are an artist, you have to strike a deal with the world's biggest labels, or gatekeepers. But *Spotify* removed that middlemen by paying artists an initial check with a royalty every time your music is streamed on *Spotify*. Furthermore, *Spotify* doesn't own the entire distribution rights of your music, the opposite is true if you sign a deal with music labels like *EMI* or *Warner Music*.

Take a look at how the new Permisssion-less model has changed the industry entirely

In 2011, the largest recorded music retailer in the world was now a digital, Internet-based platform operated by a computer company: *Apple Inc.*'s online *iTunes* Store.

- Independent labels — 22.6% (*Itunes, Apple Music, Spotify, Pandora*)
- Universal Music Group — 21.1%
- Sony Music Entertainment — 17.4%
- EMI — 14.1%
- Warner Music Group — 13.4%
- BMG — 11.4%

You are probably consuming music from one of the above streaming services today, be it *Apple Music, Spotify* or *Pandora*. You can also download the song file and listen to it again and again so long you continue to pay the streaming subscription. Once you stop paying the subscription, you cannot listen to your favorite songs from the company's ever growing repository anymore.

Since 2014, this all you can eat model has become todays norm. When was the last time you bought a CD from *EMI*? The last time I checked, my *MacBook* doesn't even come with a CD ROM. My *iPhone* connected to *CarPlay* doesn't even need to have one while getting access to millions of albums from David Bowie's 1967 album to discovering new artists like Mandolin Orange in the folk American genre.

In this new age, traditional lines that once divided singers, instrumentalists, publishers, record companies, distributors, retail and consumer electronics have been erased. If you are an independent artist, the new subscription based model will give you access to an audience of 217 monthly active listeners. It's time to tell your story and build your new fan base without permission from publishers.

CHAPTER XI BRANDING

If you look at a new brand or a Trump or an Oprah or anyone like that, these people can get rich just off their name because their name is such a powerful branding. In a business sense, you think of Trump you have to realize that they guy was among the best in the world at just branding his name. Why would you go to Trump casino, because of Trump, why would you go to Trump tower, because of Trump. When it came time to vote, they got a lot of voters just went and said Trump because they recognize the name and the name recognition paid off the same thing with the Oprah brand. Oprah would create a product with her name on something and the product would fly off the shelves. Beginning with brand rather than substance is dangerous.

But these people are also taking risks for putting the name out there, Obviously Trump is now probably hated by more than half of America .By and large, whoever takes a big chunk of the world and sticks his or her name out there, you might become a celebrity and fame has many downsides.

Thus, it's better to be anonymous and rich than to be famous and rich. But even famous and rich has a lot of downside associated with. As you're always in the public eye so accountability is quite important when you're working to build a product or even a team. When you are working in a business, we are constantly get this drilled into our heads how important it is to be part of a team.

I absolutely agree with that a lot because there is a saying from my Australian friends that the tall Poppy gets cut, so don't stick your neck out. Well, I would say that to stand out, it is really a function of getting clear accountability. We all had that experience when we went to school and got an assignment to do and there were a few people that would allow the other people to do a lot of work but take all the risks.

You can actually build credibility but you have to take risk. When you take risk, you take the risk of failure, risk of humiliation and you take the risk with your own name. Which luckily in modern society, there' no more debtors in prison than murderers. More often than not, people don't go to jail or get executed for losing other people's money but we are socially hardwired to not fail in public under our names and the people who have the ability to fail in public under their own names actually gain a lot of power.

For instance, I'll give you a personal anecdote up to until about 2013-2014 my public persona was entirely around trading and value investing and only in 2015-2017 did I start talking about philosophy and technology things and it made me a little nervous because I was doing it under my own name and they were definitely people in the industry that will send you messages in the finance sector like "what are you doin?, you're ending your career and it is stupid" but I just went with it and took the risk with unproven new tech like cryptocurrencies. When you put your name out there, you take a risk of certain things but you also get the reward and the benefits of accountability which is important.

Because that's how you are going to get leverage and you are going to get more reviews that will help potential future *Airbnbers*. It is also how you are going to get equity, like a piece of a business when you're increasing the number of property listings. Ultimately, if someone else is making a decision about alternatives, that decision is based on how replaceable your property are and if you have a uniquely designed listing, that makes you less replaceable.

On the contrary, the potential landlord you are going to pitch this idea will have to give you a quote which is the initial deposit. Look at it as a risk-based instrument. What's the worst case scenario that the property generates less than 15 booking days to break-even? All you lose is you initial deposit of say a thousand dollars.

Daily cash payout on Airbnb means you get paid everything after all the people have checked out of your property, you get paid first.

And if you are a board member of a company and the company spent too much money and has back taxes, the government will go after you personally to pay back the salaries so the employee get the most security but in exchange for that security, your employees don't have as much upside.

Next in line would be debt holders who are normally the banks. The banks will lend money to the company for operations and they need to make their fixed interest every month of every year, but they don't get much upside beyond that because they might be making 5% or 10% per year but that's where the upside is limited to capital given to business owners. And then finally when you're the equity holders of a company, you are actually going to get most of the upside and once the debt is paid off and salaries are paid off, whatever remains goes to you.

However, if there isn't enough to pay off, for some reasons, debt holders or barely enough to pay off the debt holder, which is what happens with most businesses is that most of the time the equity holders get nothing. In other words, equity holders take on a greater risk but then the risk in exchange they get nearly unlimited upside and you can do the same with all of your work.

Essentially, taking accountability for your actions is the same as taking an equity position in all of your work. You are essentially taking a greater downside risk and greater upside. But in modern society, the downside risk is not that large as you might think, even personal bankruptcy can be wiped clean by clearing out the debts. In good ecosystems, it just feels like it's a fragile thing and it could actually be a fragile example of accountability.

If you are an airplane pilot, as a captain, you're taking on accountability for the entire plane. Let's say there's something goes wrong with the aircraft and one of the engines just burst into flames mid air, you can't blame it on anyone else. You can't blame it on the steward or stewardess, you can't blame it on the co-pilot. You are the captain and you're responsible for the aircraft and if you screw up and you crash the aircraft, there are immediate consequences.

In the old days, if you are a captain of a ship, the captain of the ship was expected to go down with the ship if the ship was sinking. Literally the last person who get off was the captain so yes, accountability does come with real risks. But today, we are talking about it in a business context. If you are a business owner, you would probably be the last one to get your capital back out and you'd be the last one to get paid for your time.

So you know that the time you put in capital into the company he or she will be at risk even if a business fails, and if your names on it, that's not as bad as if it's turned out be an integrity issue like Bernie Madoff. That name is never going to be good again in the investment community, you could be Bernie's great great grandson, you are not going to go into the investment business because Bernie has ruined the family name.

These days, the accountability risk with the name happens more around integrity rather than through the economic value.

The big takeaway about accountability in modern society is that, you will be rewarded directly in proportion with your accountability.

It is also they people like Brian Krzanich, who gets rewards-eligible for $28.5 Million stock rewards without accountability, and later fired for having inappropriate relationship with an employee highlighted over the #MeToo movement.

Skin in the Game by Nassim Taleb is a required reading if I wanted to get anywhere in my own life and understand how modern systems work. Skin in the game would be near top of my list to read but yes I skin in the game goes hand-in-hand and I think accountability as a reputation. It's putting your personal reputation on the line as skin in the game, which is a simple concept and the only part of accountability that is a little counterintuitive.

We are currently socially brainwashed to not take on accountability not in a visible way but I think there are ways to take on accountability where every member of a team can take on accountability for their portion and that is how you get a well-functioning team. At the same time putting credits and losses in the correct columns. So what we are going to talk a little bit about is leverage.

THE ART OF PERSUASION IN A LOW-TRUST SOCIETY

ABC. Always be closing. But can you really be always closing in a low-trust society where information is abundant and free. Everyone in sales probably has heard of that line. You may have seen it from the 1992 film Glengarry Glen Ross, where Alec Baldwin's character treats it as gospel. Although it is taken as truth in the sale world, It's completely wrong in today's Permissionless Economy.

In fact, the 'always be closing' approach to sales in the digital economy is the enemy of persuasion. In today's low-trust society where anyone with a product and a webpage can start a Facebook or Google ad, it demands an entirely different approach.

The basic presumption behind that that infamous saying is that everything a person says or does in the course of persuading someone should be aimed purely at getting to yes. Persuasion isn't about coercing your audience to do what you want. Rather, it's about attracting them to a particular conclusion, and letting them get there on their own. Pull marketing is alway better than push marketing. In the age of innovation economy, it is much easier to sell your product with pull marketing.

One way to draw someone to your position is by engaging your audience's emotions through that most human of activities-storytelling. When told well, a great story draws people into the narrative, absorbing them in a world that is separate from their own. And once they're immersed in a story, they're far more willing to let their guard down and loosen their grip on preconceived notions.

Consider that great storytellers like Kylie Jenner with 146 million followers as of this writing, are also great truth seekers. If you can't state your message in a single, uncomplicated sentence, you might as well not have a message.

This format of identifying your goal (who are your characters, and what do they want?) the obstacle (what's in those characters' way?) And the resolution (the preferred outcome) works best in a 30 second commercial, or an in-person sales pitch, or just a conversation with a customer. You can also achieve scale with code-based leverage once your storytelling moves, connects and creates meaningful bonds with your customers.

Social media makes this easier by exposing not just the stories you tell, but your values which will compel others to adopt those same values. Once you've done that, you'll have won the customer and trust.

"Give me a Lever long enough and a place to stand and I will Move the Earth"- Archimedes

HOW TO GAIN LEVERAGE IN THE NEW AGE

Fortunes require leverage. Business leverage comes from capital, people and products with no marginal cost of replication. The reason why I'm reflecting on this Archimedes quote is not that I like putting Greek physicist quotes because you can probably look up those people's quotes. Rather it is fundamental to what I read at a young age and it had a huge impression on me.

We all know what leverage mean when we see a seesaw or a lever. We understand how that works physically but our brains are too busy to comprehend how much leverage is possible in the permission-less economy. In the old days, a pharaohs leverage is labor, and instead of me lifting rocks myself, I can have ten people lift rocks and built a tiny pyramid.

PICKING A BUSINESS MODEL WITH LEVERAGE

The question is, if you list it will they come? Famous line in the classic 1989 click "Field of Dreams" where Kevin Costner's character Ray Kinsella starts hearing voices to build a baseball diamond in his field, sacrificing all the income from his crop.

So you start hearing voices about starting an a portfolio or properties. And the voice starts to get louder and louder to take that leap of faith. When you finally hit the magic "publish" button and launch your property to the rest of the world, all day you keep refreshing your stats, page views and other metrics.

Will your listing flooded by booking requests or, Crickets? Hope is not a strategy, there is certainly no such thing as hope marketing. You spent nine months of your life after quitting your highly paid investment banking job, that voice starts to sound like a feeble dog, but you are still hesitating to take it behind the barn and shoot it.

It is an uphill battle to get attention in this world saturated with millions of other products. Sometimes there are hidden obstacle to selling- because sellers often underestimate the starting point and how wide open there are exposed to other competition. Most first time founders kind of hope people want to come and use their stuff or be their customers.

The prefect target market will be a small group of individuals congregating together served by few or no competitors. I would argue that large markets are a bad choice because it's already being served by large corporations.

Walk into any Venture Capitalist's office and tell them you are deploying a marketing strategy called 'hope' and getting 1% of of a $100 billion market, you will be laughed out of the room with no returned calls or emails.

SMALL & NICHE MARKETS

It will be much easier to dominate a niche market and gradually expand into related or adjacent markets. When creating a new product or service, there's one thing for certain- you will launch it one day.

And that day could be a success or flop.

Your property listing launch should not be a lottery ticket. This is especially applicable for high end listings with above $1,500 per night described later in this book. What does successful launches have in common? The most likely question in business is whether success comes from luck or skill. Malcolm Gladwell, who studied software billionaires, Wall Street lawyers and geniuses with IQ above 190 to find the ingredients of success and concluded that at the highest level: it always comes down to passion, talent and hard work. So how do we get the patchwork of lucky break and arbitrary advantages?

Let's consider the pattern for great product launches, *Jurassic World*.

When you turn on Discovery Channel of NatGeo, they are all talking about dinosaurs. Velociraptors, Triceratops, Brachiosaurus and of course T-Rex. If you turn on demand streaming channels, guess what? Dinosaurs. I even went painstakingly went to rent *Jurassic Park* 1,2 and 3 BlueRays to quench my dino thirst.

In 2015, the *Jurrassic World* crossed $1.5 billion worldwide (on a single week) and it became the third highest grossing film of all time. *Jurrassic World* grew so fast, it even surpassed Avatar, which took 23 days to hit $80 million. Every company starts in a unique circumstance, and every company starts with one product or service. It's about the process and beyond that, it's about 'content' and 'distribution'. Here are few things you can go months before your product launch.

1. Build a Influencer Channel

This can be people who can directly influence their network to sign up and buy your product and service. A few years ago, I built a list of 40 'influencers" in the travel niche and on launch day, with a quick email from just 2 partners, we generated more than $20k bookings on the first day. There are people out there who have an email list and some influence. Once you researched about them, friend them on social media then email them about what you are doing and invite them to become a launch partner.
For us that two partners made up of 90% of the traffic and sales so you will never know which partners but they all can help you drive traffic and eventually sales.

2. Create a 4 part automated Video Series

Product a four part video series that shares something amazing like strategies, insights, methodologies for helping you get your target audience get better results for what the experience in staying in that property provides.

The perfect indoctrination flow should look like this. The first video would be " Describe the current pain" with : 3 Proven Techniques to solve that pain"

The next video should be something like " The Simple strategy to escape the daily grind and gain pleasure immediately"

The third video may let your your audience " how to get experience Phuket in 3 simple steps "

And the fourth video should be what you are building and you are giving exclusive "VIP access " to your product at a deep discount when it goes live. You could also offer a Kickstarter-like approach to have people pledge to gain access to certain levels of your product & service you can get upfront cash while you're building it.

Remember you are taking your customer down the path with the end result, your product or service.

So don't launch into crickets. Create compelling contents, secure your distribution channels, build partnerships and spread the word.

3. DISTRIBUTION

By sending out emails or letters, you can get a few partners to help you spread the word, your partners can feel great about sharing your contents to their audience.

You will want to set a date and time where your high end property go live and let your partners know the video will go out , for instance Sept 20th at 11am EST, the product goes live! The way to do this is to dominate a small niche and market it quickly from all angles. From there, sale up toward your ambitious long-term visions. Business is like chess, to succeed, you have to study the endgame before everything else.

Distribution may not matter in fictional worlds, Peter Thiel former co founder of *Paypal* pointed out that business owners usually underestimate the importance of distribution. In this new age of permission less economy, although the 'middlemen' is out of the way, distribution will not flow magically even you have a great product.

There is a common misconception amongst first time entrepreneurs that if you have a cool product rather than thinking about distribution strategy, sales will come in. But people will not come in just because you built it. Property listing is easy, for most businesses, the main reason business come to a stall is because of poor distribution strategy.

You have to make that happen. Taylor Swift or Justin Bieber may make it look easy, but it's harder than it looks. You might be skeptical of advertising, marketing and sale. People don't like to to sold to but they like to buy. Thus, advertising might not help your buyers buy your product right away, but it will create a subtle impression which will drive sales later.

So how do you orchestrate an effective online campaign to change surface appearance of your product without changing the underlying reality?

Ideally, you should pick a business model with network effects. Most people underrate the importance of network effects in this interconnected world. The number of users on Airbnb is increasing every single day, and that means for potential visitors to your listings.

It can also mean encouraging your users to invite their friends to become users too. This is how *Facebook* or *Uber* both grew quickly. But this requires capital to achieve a chain reaction of exponential growth. For instance, Uber spends $40 for per new rider and passenger but it also achieved extraordinary growth. That said, the company that can dominate the category will have a first mover advantage with viral potential.

There are also examples like *Dropbox* giving users extra space of 500MB for every referral which helped *Dropbox* increased sign ups by 65%.

So how do you choose a business model or a choice of product that can also bring in a kind of leverage?

Next, it has to has low marginal costs. The product you produce must have low or zero marginal costs to replicate. Most software products have zero marginal cost. But in Silicon Valley, nerds are skeptical of advertising because you may think you're an exception, so it's easy to develop a false confidence in our own independence of mind. The fastest growing companies like Uber or Airbnb spend billions yearly to achieve network effects that will create scale economies described later. When you combine network effects, low marginal costs and scale economies, thats how startups appear from nowhere achieving billion dollar valuations.

WHY YOU WILL NEVER GET A BUSINESS CARD THAT SAYS SALESMAN

We live in a world where none of us wants to be reminded when we're being sold. This explains why, you will never get a business card that says "Salesperson". In fact, the very people who are in sales or marketing have titles like "Business Development". And people who sell other companies are called "Investment Bankers" and people who sell themselves are called "Politicians".

The most fundamental step to build a distribution channel is to understand it is a systematic effort to build sales funnels or the indoctrination process of getting a customer to purchase your product. The purpose of building an indoctrination process is to reframe "selling' at every level of every field in a world where all brands are competing for the same attention.

You might wish that selling your company requires little to no marketing. In the old days where you employ a few salespeople, place some magazine ads, and try to add some kind of viral functionality but it does not work anymore.

Most business fail not because of bad product but poor distribution channels. When you start a company you have to sell to potential employees and investors to hop on this ride into uncharted territory. If you happen to ask startup founders about getting early employees, rarely will you hear " The company is so great investors are lining up to invest", or " people are banging down our doors to join the company".

In Silicon Valley engineers often have the thinking of "if you built it, they will come." In reality you have to make that happen and it's harder than perceived.

So should the New Rich pursue a business that has brand effects? Or pursue a business that has network effects?

In the land of permission less economy, you can have zero marginal cost of reproduction. In other words, producing your next Youtube or Podcasts is next to free. The beauty of technology or media products is that creating another copy is free.

Once you gain a certain number of subscribers, and when someone new listens to your podcasts of Youtube Video, it doesn't cost anything for the next 100 people who watches it. Of course you gain very little profits per user in the beginner, but over time the profits can really compound when you have a large base of audience.

For example, PewDiePie is working no harder on his current Youtube videos than he was on Youtube number 1, but on Youtube number 300, he's making a million dollars from Youtube whereas for previous ones he probably make little to no money. This is an example of how zero marginal cost work in a permission less economy.

CHAPTER XII: NATURAL MONOPOLIES WITH NETWORK EFFECTS

The most powerful tech companies today has very strong network effects, scale economies and branding. You might think proprietary technology and Google's search algorithm is enough to make Google a natural monopoly.

But users themselves, are creating some value for Google. If you are using a product online for free, you are probably the product. And that's where network effect can make it very hard for other competitors who enter the space or search engine.

Yes, google might have proprietary technology that are 10 times better than it's closer substitute, that can support its monopoly, but let's just define network effects precisely.

THE INVISIBLE FORCE OF NETWORK EFFECTS

Let's just say that 1000 people in a city starts using Airbnb, each person just uses one of those 10 short term rental apps available out there. Well, you're having to switch websites all the time when a friends shares a location, it's incredibly painful.

But if 10,000 people in your city uses the same listing site, Airbnb, it would add tremendous value because data from all 10,000 will be added to the network to create better data and room recommendations.

Well now, all of sudden 10,000 people in your city uses Airbnb to search for her next vacation rental, so the next person comes in to download a new short term rental app will probably going to choose Airbnb. At some point, let's say Airbnb gets to 1 million people, it's done. It's just going to own the entire short term rental marketplace, and even people with smartphones installed with Expedia will be opting out and start using Airbnb to search for listings.

To achieve network effects, your product will have to be valuable to its very first base of users when the network is usually small. For instance, Facebook started with just a handful of Harvard students and Mark Zuckerberg built a website to allow all his classmates so sign up. Facebook's first user base was so small that most large corporations discount that to be a viable business opportunity.

Even language has network effects. Today the internet is speaking English and people from all around the world can have access to all the materials in information and it just haven't been translated into other languages.

If you only speak French or German, you would be left out of all the academic publications because from a technical education standpoint, you have to learn English to be able to read these books. Even programming languages are in English, that is why even in the entire language marketplace, the rest of the languages will be competed out.

What about China? China has created a closed off Internet but people who want to communicate on the Internet has to be forced to speak English. Today, China's wages is increasing and cheap labor is moving to countries like Indonesia and Vietnam. China Airbnb rival xiaozhu.com raised $330 million led by Jack Ma's Yunfeng Capital. Local rival includes tujia.com and in 2017 is worth north of $1billion. Alibaba is currently testing facial recognition technology in its door locks in about 40 cities.

Although Airbnb is trying to gain footing in China, it has been forced to comply with strict regulations, and host information to Chinese government agencies.

However, you can still tab into the armies of skilled industrial engineers in China who can make prototypes of your new device and build them at scale. Hardware entrepreneurs can build prototypes at lightning fast speed in place like Shenzen with direct access to thousands of factories and hundreds of thousand of engineers who help them build the next hardware at scale. Apple leverages on Chinese manufactory to the fullest, owning the entire parts suppliers and product manufacturing ecosystem.

But this book focuses on zero marginal costs of production to enable scale economies for your business.

DOES MONEY HAS NETWORK EFFECTS?

Money is a great example of network effects. The US dollar is the world's single most used currency and reserve currency. We should all be using the same money. Capital and investment flow into countries with stable money like the US dollar. This explains why people in hyper inflationary countries like Venezuela, Sudan or Zimbabwe is holding the US dollar as a reserve currency.

Even Facebook is trying to create a cryptocurrency called Libra, it will be interesting to see in the near future, even digital assets follow the law of network effects.

In sum, network effects can be powerful, but you'll never reap them unless you pick a business model with low marginal costs and scale economies, because these two tend to go hand in hand.

The ultimate form of leveraging network effects is to think about how your users, your customers, can add value to each other. For example, the more people download the Uber App, the more it benefits drivers of Ubers and thus encouraging more drivers to sign up to be an Uber driver. So you can be at the beach or sleeping at night while your customers are adding value to each other.

How to get Optionality and how do you price future income

Let's take a look at Net Present Value of NPV. To get an idea of NPV is when you get a gauge of the stream of payments you expect to get in the future what is it worth today.

The question is starting the next Airbnb that will be worth $1 billion is harder than it looks, because a company could create a lot of value without becoming very valuable itself.

Take the airlines industry for instance, the average "profit per passenger" of the seven largest U.S. airlines was $17.75 in 2017 — for just a one-way flight according to the Wall Street Journal. Compare this to a Tech company like *Google*, the company brought in $136 billion in 2018 verses $32 billion for all airlines combined. *Google's* parent company Alphabet is making so much money that its now worth more than three times of all airlines in the U.S.

CHAPTER VIII SCHELLING POINT IN BUSINESS AND AIRBNB LISTINGS

Thomas Schelling a nobel prize winning economist who introduced the idea of focal points in 1960. Schelling's original example was if two strangers were trying to meet in New York on a particular day, but not knowing a time and place. Both of them can't communicate so both of them will have to pick an arbitrary date.

Not knowing the place, many people will successfully pick the Grand Central Station at mid day with almost no information. You might pick other places like Time Square but it's highly unlikely.

When Schelling points are applied to business, an organization with clear strategic goals allow everyone to make co-ordinated decisions without input on very decision. Thus, Schelling points can be found in business, art, politics and even Airbnb listings in your neighborhood. Let's say you have two direct competitors pricing similar property to yours at $125 and $100, without communication, the two competitors would eventually agree on the price of $115. Focal points can also be highly useful in negotiations, because we can really trust on the algorthims within the Airbnb platform.

THE POWER OF COMPOUND INTEREST

We haven't yet uncovered the secrets of life. We talked about compound interest in a business sense but not relationships. Most relationships especially good relationships compound over time. Whether it's professional or romantic, and life gets easier because you understand that person and you don't have to keep guessing.

Systematic knowledge how having worked with someone say for twenty years, you will develop a mutual trust unless they screw you over. What if you could prolong business relationships to a certain point we don't even need legal contracts, and all we need is a handshake? However, good relationship takes time to develop.

For instance, if a friend and I started a company and things are not working out, so we both have to be reasonable to think about the next steps. Whether to design a new business model or to shut the company down but we have to be reasonable about it. Since we have mutual trust, it's going all add up and makes it easier even if we decide to start another business venture.

THE EFFORT TO BUILD A SMALL BUSINESS IS THE SAME AS BUILDING A LARGE ONE

Companies are like countries, it require the same amount of effort to run one. Whether you are the guy running a chain of three Japanese restaurants in town, working about 100 hours per week day and night, hiring and firing people in highly stressful environments, it can take a lot of effort to get the first things right.

On the other hand, you see companies worth $10- $50 billion. The truth is, the takes the same amount of work and effort whether you are running a nice restaurant or a billion dollar startup.

How you can charge more? Businesses make billions from one secret- Consumer Surplus

First, businesses will have to understand how consumer surplus and producer surplus works.

Consumer surplus the the difference between the price that consumer is currently paying dnd the price they we willing to pay. For example, I you would pay $5 for a cup of coffee, but you can buy it at other places for $3, your consumer surplus is $2.

I get a lot of joy from my morning Starbucks coffee by paying about $3 for a cup of Americano, however is Starbucks rolls out a new say , Shakerato Bianco espresso shaken with ice, Demerara syrup with 1/2 sweet cream for $10, I would pay for it.

And *Starbucks* knows that because they can price their coffee at $20.79 to target people willing to pay for it and thats is consumer surplus. For those reasons, *Starbucks* created *Starbucks Reserve* which claimed that they tend bring different customer experience to a whole new level. To provide a whole new experience, a firm could charge a whole new level of price- this means charging the consumer the highest price they are willing to pay.

Cheap is not marketing. To gain market power, you could advertise to create brand loyalty and this will make the demand for your product or service more inelastic. In competitive markets, you have to keep prices relatively low to gain an initial base of clients. Once you have done that, you should gauge the consumer surplus of your consumers. Try testing with higher price points on Airbnb during peak holiday seasons.

If you have first mover advantage in a less competitive market, consumer surplus would be less but this can lead to higher producer surplus and greater inequality.

It's good thing to keep in mind as a business owner, you could create various price points for your customer base. *Marriott International* for example might be the biggest hotel chain in the world, but they are generating billions from consumer surplus for brands like *JW Marriott, St Regis, W Hotels*. Because a lot of people are willing to pay more than what *Marriott* charges.

Producer surplus is when there are more sellers producing the same product or service in a market. This can be measured as the difference between the market price and cost of production. The different between consumer surplus and producer surplus is that the highest price a consumer is willing to pay and the lowest price a producer would be willing to accept.

When there is a lot of producers entering a space, the price will reach equilibrium eventually, as described earlier guided by the *Schelling point*.

A lot of entrepreneur make the mistake of pricing their product cheap. Again, by understanding consumer surplus, going cheap on your brand development could only lead to a disconnect with potential customers. In some cases, the business might fail. Marc Andreessen, a prominent VC based in Silicon Valley who co founded Netscape in the 90s has two words of advice for startups: *Raise Prices*.

He added most companies are really struggling because they are not charging enough for their product and it is a conventional wisdom in Silicon Valley is that to succeed, you have to price is as low as possible or even give it away for free.

When Airbnb listers are too hungry to eat for not charging enough for their listings, they won't be able to purchase good furnitures or afford to hire professionals to do interior designs to spice up the property. It makes sense to lower prices to increase occupancy rate but when you keep lowering prices, it will only be a race to the bottom.

The question you should be asking, if your listing is so great, why people are not willing to pay more for it? Therefore, assessing consumer surplus as the first step is important to build a sustainable business and all businesses, from *Amazon* to *Starbucks* to *Tesla* generate consumer surplus.

Think about the extra value you can provide for your customers instead of slashing prices, a problem often called 'too hungry to eat' because you don't want to find yourself struggling in a red ocean. If you think *Marriott International* Luxury Brands are designed to provide a lot of value for the price with premium pricing strategy and product differentiation including brands like *St. Regis*, the luxury collection, *W Hotels, the Ritz-Carlton, Bulgari* Hotels & resorts and *JW Marriott.*

Imagine creating an Airbnb list of properties spanning the world from the mist iconic hot spots to the ultimate undiscovered gems, the breadth and depth of a luxury portfolio that uniquely positions you to cater to the increased demand of rapidly-expanding cadre of affluent travelers. Even Tina Edmundson, global brand officer of Marriott International said in a statement: "With luxury travel up nearly 50% over the past five years, we see a long runway for growth at the high-0end."

The average price of an *iPhone* is $1,400 where most Indians make less than that in a month. In third quarter 2019, *iPhones* generated $26 billion and all around the world shipments fell 11 percent except India, sales of *iPhones* in India actually grew 19 percent Year over year. If slashing prices were the solution, there will be less companies go out of business.

Remember, your customer is willing to pay more than you think and you have to find a way to gauge that. What if companies start using data to gauge consumer surpluses? In China, people are going cashless. Companies like *Alibaba* and *Tencent* have proven how lucrative data mining can be. Everything transaction linked to millions of smartphones may have created some of China's home grown internet giants and it will never stop there. The deeper you can get into data like these, the easier it will be to gauge consumer surplus in your small market niche. It's a distinction that separates companies that grow big and companies that struggle to win more clients.

It will be easier to market to your existing client base than to score new clients. Going deep means understanding your clients and building walls around your business, insulating yourself from the economic bloodshed of price competition. When two companies went into the same niche, they may take different approaches. Throwing tons of money into attaining scale is not only expensive, but logistically taxing endeavor. Instead think about creating an entirely new category, a product that is at least 10 times better than your competition.

IMMUTABLE LAWS OF BRANDING

The immutable laws of branding by Al Ries is a topic I always revisit. If you compare American Brands and Japanese brands, top hundreds companies in the U.S have an annual sales of $3.2 trillion. And for Japan the top hundred companies had sales of $2.6 trillion, not much different but there is a big difference in profits.

The net profit for top hundred American companies is 6.2 percent while the top hundred Japanese companies just 0.8 percent of sales. Korean companies is even faring more poorly, the sixty three largest companies in Korea with sales over $409 billion has a net loss of 0.4 percent of that sales. The answer is clear, less is more and putting your brand on everything will destroy your brand. Having ten very profitable listings is better than having twenty that is barely breaking even.

Is it an accident to find people lining up to buy the new *iPhone*? Or Steve Jobs is one great marketing genius who understood this law of branding? Most businesses make the mistake of creating more products when customers are not rushing out to buy your product. You will never see people rush out of their homes lining up to buy a *Hyundai* refrigerator or a *Mitsubishi* Pickup truck. Don't laugh, this is the way most large corporations think and in actuality, its eroding the core brand.

In sum, the marketplace do not need endless line extensions but the market is eager to give you money if you can create a brand in a particular niche where they are needed. Your consumers are smarter than you think, before you launch your next product line, do a survey and ask your existing customers what will they think if you launch this next product. Your existing customers will give you an insights for you to make high level business decisions on whether to stay with the current product line and continue to build your brand or to launch the next one. As an entrepreneur, I have to always remind myself whenever I feel the urge to create sub brands, that is, if I had to create one, I am chasing the market, not building the brand.

To understand sub brands is what leading marketers like to call the concept of masterbranding. For instance, sub branding is creating a subsidiary or secondary brand which reflects the identity of the main brand, like *Holiday Inn* to *Crowne Plaza* or *Mustang* to Ford. What is Ford then? Ford is a megabrand.

According to Gresham's law of marketing, sub brands can actually destroy the main brand, it can take your company to the opposite direction. People don't check in to Holiday Inn and expect luxury services. Imagine if *LVMH* creates a sub brand, or a less costly and more casual line of leather products. It would completely destroy the luxury perception in customer's mind.

However, if you create a more luxury brand, that will elevate your customer's perception. This can be exemplified by the secrets of *Lexus's* success. In the 70s and 80s Toyota image to the world is reliable yet cheap automobiles. In the 90s *Toyota* decided to launch the *Lexus* brand, now synonymous with the world of luxury. In a short period, Lexus's sales even superseded *Mercedes Benz* and *Cadillac* in the US. Very quickly *Honda* and *Nissan* followed suit with its *Acura* and *Infiniti* brand.

For tech brands this can also be true. *Uber Black* for example, where passengers can request for a larger SUV or more luxury car for their propensity to pay. Recall that all businesses generate consumer surplus. There are trillions of dollars in the market in consumer surplus through people's willingness to pay for convenience or pay for your product as a signaling good.

That's something to think about when building a portfolio of Airbnb properties. It was true for Gene Dexter, of the Dexter Experience to lease a Villa in Phuket called Villa of 1000 Smiles #3 Penthouse for $225 per night on Airbnb with 80% occupancy rate.

Most successful new age of capitalists who create the most valuable kind of company maintains a very strong action bias. This leads to creating optionality in a code-based world that the upside can be so great with limited downsides. Silicon Valley has learned to never look down on a slob with hoodie wearing flip flops. Just because he look like a slob, if he succeeds, he might become the next Mark Zuckerberg or Jeff Bezos.

In the Airbnb Equation, you have got to keep a lookout for every possibility and opportunities because the upside is unlimited and the downside is limited. More so with financial assets and instruments in the modern age. This is why so many why so many Airbnb entrepreneur don't appear to have the marketing budget like bigger hotel chains, but they built a superior product and the product itself is kind of distribution.

It is also important to identify the most important target customers first to validate your property listing potential. The viral potential should come next. Instead of acquiring more users at random with a limited budget, get your most valuable users first. The most obvious market segment in the early days of Facebook was the thousands of students in campuses who want to connect with other students. Facebook made that effortless, but the connections were too infrequent so Facebook understood they needed a smaller niche market segment with a higher usage of social networking. We needed a platform and a smaller niche market segment with higher social interaction- a segment Facebook found in Harvard and other campuses who frequently send texts and comments through Facebook's site.

How do you communicate your company's product to potential customers? Selling starts when you list your first property. Airbnb capitalist have to explain why their listing is so great travellers are willing to show up at their door with their luggages ready to check in. Entrepreneurs should never assume the public will admire your listing without a good photos and description.

Most of the time, founders who can sell with good photography will be able to sell to everyone because camera angles is often a distribution strategy to attract potential customers to place a reservation. Next you are going to need to rely on the interior design of your property to get you across the line with new bookings. The returns you reap from the effort you put into thinking, planning and executing the interior design or your Airbnb listing will compound over time.

Now on the other end of the spectrum will be the 'crazy zones'. There are plenty of listings who created our of the crazy zone. And while you can always get a few clients to book your listing, it's very difficult to convince the masses to take action at all on the left or right.

		Neutral		Polarity	
Crazy	Prolific	Main Stream	Prolific		Crazy
Luxury Tuscan Villa- $3,500 per night- Malibu, California	SeaShell House- Isla Mujeres, Mexico	Comfortable Room with Private Bath- New York City	Off-Grid House- California, USA		Snow Igloo - Pelkosenniemi
2810 Private Estate - $3,000 per night -Las Vegas	Secluded in-town tree house- Atlanta, USA	Clean Separate Studio in New York	Mini Loft, Rome, Daily		Smallest House in the World- Boston
Wine Country Villa, $2,000 per night- Calistoga	Mushroom Dome Cbin in Aptos, California	Affordable too near LGA airport	Beautiful Tree House- Bali, Indonesia		Glamorous home w/Tesla included
Mountaintop Retreat in Idledale, $2,500 per night- Colorado	Casa Barthel in Tuscany, Italy	Cozy 1 bedroom Apartment- Singapore	Pirates of the Carribean Getway- California, USA		1964 Piper PA-28 Airplane house- Phoenix
Vintage Mansion with	Retro home with	Safe, cozy & minutes to	Dome Cabin- Cali-		Crypt hotel with

THE AIRBNB EQUATION

Staff, $3,000 per night- Vermont	Danish Design+ bikes- Copenhagen	LAX- Los Angeles	fornia, USA	Built in actual Crypt- Maine
Private Estate in Santa Fe, $4,200 per night- New Mexico	Emblematic plaza Chueca- Portugal	Downtown San Francisco Apt- Marina Piers, San Francisco	Tuscan Treehouse - Monferrato, Italy	Cozy mud hut- Portland, Oregon
Brooklyn Brownstone, $8,000 per night- New York	Joshua Tree House- Joshua Tree, California	Private Room in Cozy Family House-Sydney, Australia	Modern Glass Tree House- Florence, Italy	The bed in a Cave- Shaanxi, China

GETTING YOUR FIRST 10 CUSTOMERS

Once you have signed a one year lease, it's time to start promoting it. Every entrepreneur should plan how to execute a distribution strategy, and how does your listing fit in the marketplace. For starters, if your niche you are targeting are people in your sub market, start becoming part of those communities and start participating in those groups. Ask questions, look for ways to add value to the community instead of posting spam messages which will likely drive people away instead of closer to your brand.

Most Facebook groups are a congregation of people with very specific interests in the niche you are focusing on. In any case if you decided to run online paid advertising, get some insights about what are the number one question your community has? You can also create a link to a survey form and if you prefer to not spend money at the early stages, social media groups can give you some intel about what works well and what doesn't.

The mistake most entrepreneurs make today is they start looking for their first property to list, find one that looks good and start building their portfolio from there without tracking customers data. The problem is you will be stepping into someone else's arena and instead of capturing a market niche, you will find yourself competing against larger competitors with more capital in a very red ocean.

If you can't create a unique experience for a small market, you'll be caught swimming in a very red ocean with vicious competition. That said, if you can't dominate a sub market, the sweet spot to to carve out a niche where you will impact the most lives and make the most money.

Don't create boring properties : Your customers must be fascinated with the listing you create. Like a secluded intern 1 Double Bed treehouse in Atlanta that lists for $370 per night. Occupancy rate 95%. And it is previously named Airbnb's #1 Most Wished-For listing world wide.

Airbnb capitalist effectively courted the first few customers, but they often forgot about producing great products. Those who stayed relevant will be the ones that are highly prolific.

Here's the description of the property:

The treehouse has a Southern nature - gracious, calming, and comfortable.
Centrally located within the heart of intown Atlanta, the treehouses are a hidden gem. The subject of TV and magazine features including the Today Show, "Treehouse Masters: Ultimate Treehouse IV", Architectural Digest, Travel + Leisure, Harper's Bazaar, and numerous others, they are often described as being the most relaxing, romantic, dreamy and unique place you'll ever stay. What could be better than falling asleep in the trees and waking up to birds singing around you--all within the city limits?

The treehouse consists of 3 separate areas - Mind, Body and Spirit - each connected by rope-bridges. Descriptions of the 3 rooms are below.

Mind - The Sitting Room: Antique furnishings and artifacts including 80 year old windows of pressed butterfly wings, a plaster cast of a Siberian Tiger paw, fossils, a couch and chairs, its a great place to read or talk and has a balcony overlooking an acre of lush woods...

Body - The Bedroom: Sleeps 2. What could be better than a great bed up in the trees? The super comfortable double bed is outfitted with the world's best bedding: Parachute. These cozy linens are made of 100% long-staple Egyptian cotton and pure Linen. They're Oeko-Tex certified, meaning no harmful chemicals or softening synthetics have been used. You'll have your best night's sleep ever here at the Treehouse! The bed is equipped with wheels so it can either be inside the room or rolled out onto a platform that overlooks the stream below. Haiku Fan from Big Ass Fans is silent and better than an air conditioner to keep you cool in summer. The mattress has a warmer for cool nights and the tin roof makes rain storms something to be enjoyed.

Spirit - The Hammock Deck: Open to the elements and immersed in thick greenery, the deck surrounds the spirited "Old Man", a 165 year old Southern Short-Leaf Pine tree--the largest of the 7 trees that support the treehouse suite and watch over its guests.

It's part of being a pioneer and it's not just exciting to build a most wished listing but to explore new fields and to recognize there is tremendous consumer surplus in the marketplace, people willing to pay a premium for your creativity.

There is nothing wrong with producing marginal better listings, but if you want to fit your message into the sweet spot of the prolific zone, you have to be prolific. For example, if a Tiki Moon Villas in Laie for $2,000 per night. While some of these listings may be good in increasing occupancy rate, I'd argue that others are flat-out boring. If you plan to charge a premium price, it's all about how you create that experience for your customers.

Now think about the vision you want to create for your listing. What do your people really want? How can you capture that in a simple calling you could put on the Title of your listing? Consumers are less good at making sense of what they want. Visionaries are the opposite, they excel at creating something people didn't know they want.

Good stories can be really simple. As you craft your story, the more authentic the better, there can be layers of complexity but at the core they are very simple. You can share a story whether it is 60 seconds video or a 200 words description.

TOWARD PLEASURE

To win the hero may be trying the win the hearts of early adopters, or they may want to win fame, money and gain prestige. Humans are always looking for ways to increase their statuses. To Retrieve- the traveller wants to obtain something and bring the experience back to their home countries.

AWAY FROM PAIN

To escape the traveller wants to move away from pain that is upsetting them or causing pain.

The story describes the journey to achieving the desire. But in all good stories, the traveller is actually on two journeys- the one that everyone sees (Journey of Achievement) and one that is hidden (Journey of Transformation). The bonds journey might not be obvious but it is the key to make the whole experience more interesting.

THE JOURNEY OF ACHIEVEMENT:

This is the first journey, a smart capitalist will put themselves in the travelers shoes and know that she has an end goal in mind, which is to escape from her daily corporate work life and have the best experience while staying in one of your listings. There's a visible goal with a finish line that everyone can see. It is also the reason the hero sets out on the journey in the first place and the audience is rooting for your customer to accomplish their journey. While this journey is what drives the traveller forward, the second journey is actually more important because if the traveller never actually achieves his end desire, it became a transformational journey that he's been on throughout the vacation.

CUSTOM PRICING STRATEGY

I do not recommend using a third party pricing agent because they don't really understand your neighborhood. Your first listing during the first three months are the most important because Airbnb's algorithm favors new listings to keep their giant machine moving. It means your new listing will get good traffic and it's important to maximize that bookings and get good reviews. If you post lousy photos with a generic description and priced it too highly, you will find it harder to get bookings going forward.

1. **Don't risk a Block of Five Days over a Single Day Booking**

If you have a five night vacancy over a single night vacancy, drop that single night because you don not want to risk losing the five day vacancy.

2. CHARGE 10-20% LESS FOR DATES THAT ARE A WEEK OUT

The reason a full-time entrepreneur focus on the potential profit they spend hosting their properties. Think of this as a business on a higher level. Calculate the per hour cost vs per hour cleaning because say your per hour income with ten listings is $250 per hour, it is clear to outsource your cleaning and maintenance for $20 per hour. The most successful entrepreneurs know how to optimize their time by minimizing the burden of these tasks. Time is your most valuable commodity and it is not replenish-able.

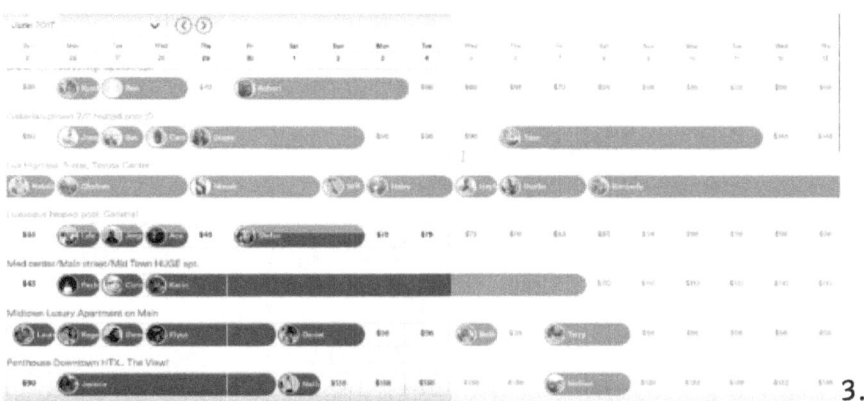

3. Reset the price based on availability of your listing.

When you have a listing of 10 of more properties, you can hire a Virtual Assistant which is widely available on freelancer sites like upwork.com to execute your custom pricing strategy.

There is a world of possibilities out there, just as Elon Musk brought the *Model 3* electric sedan to the masses, you can use virtual assistance to bring five star services within reach of each man, woman and child. Now, thats the power of the internet. Don't limit yourself, just ask your virtual assent if something is possible, accounting books, changing pricing of your listings based on competitor analysis, create compelling Airbnb descriptions, create personalized welcome notes. Just ask your virtual assistance. What virtual assistants can't do? They can't do anything that would require our physical presence. But you would be surprise as to how small a set of tasks that is in this day and age. You can instruct your virtual assistant to text your cleaning agency to see if everything is handled properly.

Here's an example of a listing by a Freelancer on Upwork.com

- Market Research
- Business plans, industry analysis, market assessment reports, preparing descriptions
- Reports and newsletters
- Legal research, analytics, website development, check with Inland Revenue to find out if listing is subject to income tax
- Search engine optimization, maintaining and updating Airbnb listings
- Managing procurement processes

You can have a virtual assistant from Bangalore or Philippines for less than $15/hour to have created a system that runs your Airbnb hotel chain.

Here are a few other entrepreneurs custom requests
- Reminding guests a day before with check in info, maps, transportation options
- Charting a dinner plan with local restaurant recommendations
- Charting a diet plan with local ordering groceries based on specific diet plan
- Finding a parking slot for your guest in some city even before they check in

- Ordered Organic Soap, Fresh flowers, new towels and linens based on your specifications online for premium listing in Phuket.
- Filing a claim on Airbnb for damages done by guest in the Resolution Center, making sure guest respond within 72 hours
- Electronic access card for entry and exit
- Change of Electronic pin on WIFI locks when guest checks out
- Texting guest with new Lock Digital Pin 3 hours before their check in time.
- Email detailed weekly report break-even analysis per each listing

START SMALL AND THEN SCALE IT INTO A BIG BUSINESS

The goal is to build a massive lean and agile hotel chain management system, something called the Just-in-time manufacturing system used by *Toyota* to reduce costs and decrease waste. This will build an automatic barrier to entry against competition and that's an important one. In other words, you should get into a business where listing property number 20 is cheaper than number 5. The two things any world class entrepreneurs understand is cash flow and time. With these two things, a lot of other things can be made possible. Without them, nothing is possible.

And of course, scale economies. In the theory of Basic Economics, the more you produce something, the cheaper it gets to make it. A lot of businesses today already have this but how do you achieve scale economy in an ever increasingly competitive world? The goal is simple: to create an automated machine that generates cash without consuming more of your time.

The important metric you should track will be the cost per completed task. If you are hiring an Indian VA for the first time, set an hour cap for three simple task so they don't spend 24 hours on one task. How do you know which to choose? It comes from hiring a few at first and you will find yourself sharpening your communication skills to determine which results driven VA is best for you. "Excellent" English is a must and some phone calls will be required to request a change of date, replacement if there are booking related issues.

If you are an effective person but do not communicate clearly with your VA, you are giving him a license to waste time. Some tasks can be easily done but some requires your VA to use Airbnb's Resolution Center to mediate a dispute. Set an order of importance. Your response time on Airbnb might affect future listings, so make sure your VA is able to respond with sufficient time. By end of the week, request for a weekly report with response time, tasks completed.

So how do you communicate with an effective email? Here's an example sent to an Indian VA which clearly explains your objective and end goal. Identify your top five time-consuming tasks and five personal tasks you could assign your VA to save you time and effort.

Hi Diya,

Thank you for accepting the work and let's start the work with the following tasks

- Research on existing neighborhood for the listing _____ the median price (based on furnishings, 1BedRoom, 1 kitchen studio, proximity to train station etc.)
- Open the zipped folder and upload them. Create compelling description and send draft back to me for approval
- Check average ratings for past 10 bookings and execute custom pricing based on the guideline as attached Please advise the number of hours required to complete the above tasks. If any of the tasks cannot be done, please inform me.

If you agree to the above, please reply and confirm the completion of the above tasks. The deadline will be ____ to reply before end of day EST Thursday and reported weekly report is end of day EST Monday.

Best,
Terrence

Once you can gauge the income per listing every mont from your property listings. Calculate the profit margin per listing and your revenue-per-employee. If you are generating $30,000 per month from your automated portfolio with two Virtual Assistance. Your annual revenue-per-employee is $180,000. Not bad at all...

It is also important to keep track of setup costs, per-unit costs and breakeven level. You can also create the property description yourself, often via paraphrasing and combining points from several superheats on your property.

When Wayne Huizenga coped the organizational chart of *McDonalds* and trend *Blockbuster* into a billion dollar corporate giant before getting disrupted by Netflix, the secret is starting with an end in mind. Of course in our case is not to create a Fortune 500 company but rather a business that bothers us as little as possible. So let's look at the architecture we are designing that will put us out of the machine (so we are not caught working in the business) and put us on top of the whole framework.

THE ANATOMY OF AUTOMATION
The Airbnb Equation Virtual Architecture

The system is the solution. This is a simplified version of what an automated architecture looks like including sample costs. You can build your own by using this structure and branch it out as your virtual organization grows. This will also be your blueprint for signing a self-sustaining cash flow positive system. The two pillars to building a self-sustaining virtual architecture is to ask the following questions:

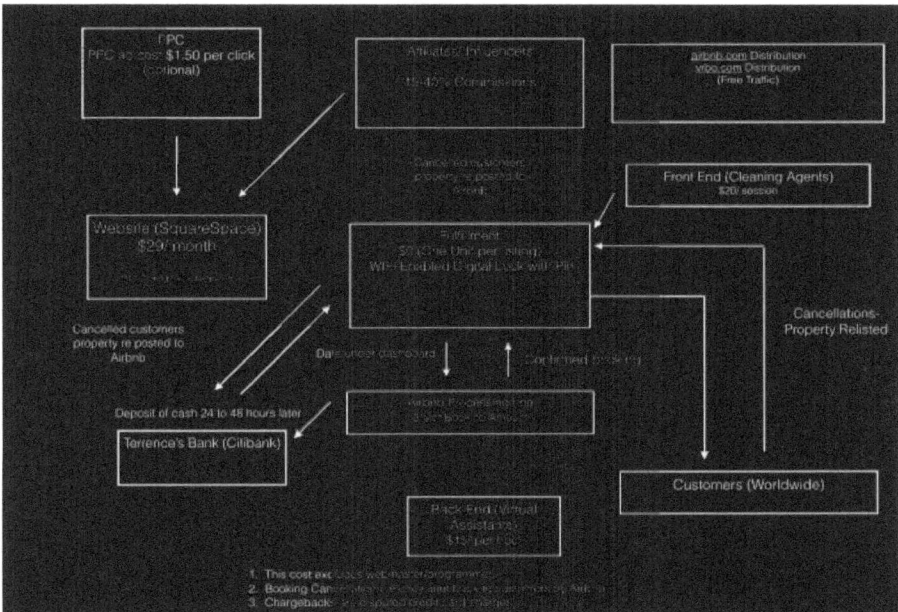

1.) Will your contract companies or freelancers you hire a specialist in the task? You can replace any of your freelancers if they don't meet your tasks so accountability for each member is important here.

2.) Will your outsourced workers be willing to communicate amongst themselves to solve problems? When you built a system that is running smoothly like a well oiled machine, this architecture can be scalable. By scalable I mean you could have 20 listings and handle 100 bookings per week with little or not effort from you.

PHASE ONE: 0-20 BOOKINGS PER WEEK

The first phase is to do it all yourself so you understand the flow on the Airbnb site for both general questions and booking confirmations or cancellations. This is important to understand because you will be training your virtual assistance how to handle those later in an online FAQ. You can also screenshot the conversations of your first 30 interactions with customers and build a list of FAQs. Answer all texts promptly because it will affect your response rate, download the Airbnb app if necessary. Personally hand the keys for your first few customers and access the analytics on Airbnb's dashboard to understand your target customers. Start to find local cleaning agencies and narrow down the agents who will agree not to charge you a deposit fee or monthly minimums. The cleaning cost should not exceed the cost of your cleaning fee you set on Airbnb.

PHASE TWO: MORE THAN 20 BOOKINGS PER WEEK

Next, use the FAQ you build and post it to your website and continue to add more answers to commonly asked questions. Get at least 5 good ratings and maintain a good rating and ask for recommendations if possible. Limit communications to Airbnb texts. Communicate with your cleaning agents and ask for net 30 days terms payment for their services they rendered on your properties. Have your cleaning agent restock supplies by letting them know where you placed them in the property like toilet paper, soap, fresh towels, extra linens etc. You can also get them to take photos on their smartphone once service is rendered and send them to your VA so they can make sure everything is in good order according to your system.

PHASE THREE: MORE THAN 50 BOOKINGS PER WEEK

Now you are a baller. You will have enough cash flow to talk to the next property owner and show them your portfolio of listings and how you can ensure their properties will be in good management. Set up a Slack group for all your VA, cleaning agents, private chefs, drivers so that information flow seamlessly. Interview them about their expectations and the experience they have. Don't get total beginners. Remember, you are running it like a big business now and your judgement is important. You can even get a 800 number and post it on your website for high end listing with 24 hours outsourced call centers. The phone can also have a programmed IVR and should be answered within four or five rings.

Not all customers are the same. Usually you will find that customers who pay for more, for example $1,500 per night listings will require less maintenance. The best customers are those who spend the most and complain the least. But you should not skimp on creating that unique customer experience. Customer service is not becoming a personal concierge but to understand their problems, interests, likes and recommend them good solutions. For instance, if one of your high net worth client luggages was lost and she is still waiting for a call from the airline customer service. Your customer service team should offer her to check for her by calling the airline and solve it in the fastest manner possible. If a client forgot to bring a tie for his conference tomorrow, your customer service team ask for the color of the tie and size, call the nearest tailor, get someone on the ground pick it up and place it on the dining table before breakfast is served the next day.

The art of automation means minimizing the number of decisions your customers have to make and eliminate time wasting decisions you have to make like dealing with customer complaints and problem customers.

In other words, your time should be spend smart testing, smart positioning and brilliant marketing campaigns. Once you have a process in place, fine tune it and go with the flow and then remove yourself from the equation.

GETTING THE 5 STAR RATING

After creating a system to automate your processes, now it's time to set your listings up to solidify your place as a five star host for future guests. Airbnb guest don't usually expect a five star hotel treatment, but every little things you do that exceed their expectation can really move the needle of your ratings.

1. Hotel Grade Quality Linens

Put yourself in your guests shoes. After a seven hour flight on a business trip and a long day of travelling, you finally checked in to your Airbnb accommodation and desperately needed some sleep for your business conference tomorrow. You lie down in your bed with sheets that felt like paper with bed bugs. Nobody likes sleeping on cheap and thin sheets, certainly not your guests. This is not something you should skimp when it comes to your vacation rental listing. While you don't have to spend a fortune on quality linens, just make sure they are comfortable and thick enough. Check if your towels or linens needed some replacement every 6 months. You can also put this as a reminder into your calendar to get maid cleaning services to check the state of your sheets.

2. BASIC SUPPLIES

For one bed room apartments with kitchen stoves, these are dozen of items we often overlook that will make your guests happy. Thus, stocking the following items up will be a good idea.

- Toilet paper, facial tissues, paper towels
- Basic cooking ingredients like salt, seasoning and cooking oil
- Cookware like pots, skillets and utensils
- Cleaning basics like dish soap, laundry detergent

You can also text your cleaning team to let them know where to find these items so they can restock them during their next visit.

3. PERSONALIZED TOUCHES

Simple touches that grab the attention of unsuspecting guests goes a long way. They will likely reciprocate with a great review. Here's a few things to set you apart from your competition giving them more reasons to leave you a five star review

- Personalized Welcome Notes, you can print a quick and meaningful welcome note
- Hotel-Style Bed Folding, so called hotel-esque turndowns you can instruct your cleaning service to do it for you
- Mini Toiletries for your guest
- Welcome plate. You can place some fresh apples or a bottle of drink or something else you find locally.

4. PERSONALIZED REMINDER TEXTS

Send a reminder text a day or so into their stay to ensure everything going smoothly. Offer assistance like how to get to your place cheaply with public transit routes and so on.

GOING BEYOND FIVE STAR RATING

During the HIBT Summit, Airbnb's Joe Gebbia sat down with Guy Raz explaining the different kind of experiences you can create for your guests. What if you could create an experience beyond 5 star for high end property listings that is priced above $500 per night?

THE 5 STAR EXPERIENCE

You check in, you find a hand written note on the table with a bottle of wine, with recommendations of local restaurants and also reservation for two for dinner tonight and also places to visit options for your guest to for their next two days in town.

THE 6 STAR EXPERIENCE

You arrive at the airport, a driver greets you with your name picks you up and sends you to your house. You check in, with a bottle of champaign and welcome note. A personal chef asking your for your choice of dinner.

THE 7 STAR EXPERIENCE

You arrive at the airport, a driver greets you with your name picks you up and sends you to your house. You check in, with a bottle of champaign and welcome note. A personal chef asking your for your choice of dinner. A car is waiting for you for your appointment with your business associate in town and then to your pre-booked free concert ticket to your favorite music band with backstage pass after the business appointment.

When your gears start to click, investors can hear that, and you can potentially start to raise funding to scale your business to the next level.

" The first rule of any technology used in business is that automation applied to an efficient operation will magnify the efficiency. The second is that automation applied to an inefficient operation will magnify the inefficiency."
Bill Gates Co-founder of Microsoft

LICENSING YOUR SYSTEM

You can also license your system or get a cut from existing property owners to help increase their income from Airbnb. Fees can be one-time and paid up front or revenue-sharing based (5-10% of net revenue per booking, for example)

Let's assume you know a millionaire property owner with 2 beachfront mansions in which he stays only for 2 months per year during summer. You are already having a portfolio of listings, and want to promote and generate cash flow for the property owner for the rest of 10 months of the year. If you executed the system and strategies explained in this book, you will know more about managing a vacation property more than 80% of real estate brokers. If you can summarize the service and cash flow projection you can generate for the owner, you now have a high end listing where you can take half of the profits per day like the 20 Most Expensive Airbnb listings in 2019

- Nafsika Estate, Megalochori, Santorini, Greece – $9,255.
- Stein Eriksen Condo, Park City, Utah – $8,839. ...
- Tuscany, Italy – $6,525. ...
- Kailua-Kona, Hawaii – $4,900. ...
- Tsheshepe Safari Lodge, Welgevonden Game Reserve, Limpopo, South Africa – $4,500. ...
- New Orleans, Louisiana – $4,000. ...
- All Together Now, Key West, Florida – $3,732.

Use the Airbnb Equation to build a list of potential listings and aim for listings that can be rented out for above $2,000. Even if you can rent out two out of five of the high end listings above, assuming you take 50% of the Airbnb Income, thats $7,890 per month for just one night! Our goal is qualified high net worth clients, so we do not want to offer something "lowly priced" or otherwise attract people curious who are unlikely to place a reservation. Interestingly enough, you can find some those premium listing on Airbnb that have above 50% occupancy per month! Talking about being prolific, you can also post them with a combination of digital ads or an Instagram account that shows high end property photos. If you mix it with some of your mainstream listing like Comfy 1BR Queen Size Bed that goes for $100 per night, it defeats the purpose of creating a premium listing social media account. The problem? It's mainstream.

The old capital, the upper class with two or three mansions or castles with thoroughbred greyhound dogs running around their estates are characterized as being well-established in one place. Mark Zuckerberg might own ten properties across four locations: Palo Alto, California, San Francisco, Lake Tahoe, and Kauai Island, Hawaii. His gigantic $100 million property in Hawaii along the North Shore of Kau'i. Tech billionaires might not need their properties to be listed as a vacation rental. But there are thirty six millionaires around the world today, and they own nearly half of total wealth. A recent report by Credit Suisse finds there are 2.3 million new millionaires added every year and the 36 millionaires, controls 46% of wealth of the world. What if you could give the rest of 1 billion people a taste of living like a millionaire for $1,500?

The Airbnb Equation allows you as the New Rich to have more elusive power than simple cash- unrestricted mobility. The key is to create proper leverage and implement the quantifiable business profits with under utilized assets you can find all around the world.

To get an accurate indicator of premium listings viability, you could target annual corporate retreats, don't ask people if they would buy- ask them to buy.

Research: Look at the competition and create a more-compelling offer on your premium listing with a basic one-three page website (you can do this on squarespace.com with one to three hours without coding skills, or just hire an Indian web developer for less than $500)

Test: Test the offer using Facebook ads with compelling photos (with detailed targeting, set it to five days with active observation.

Divest or Invest: Cut losses with losers and scale up marketing budget for winners. Can you tell a story by posting a video on your Youtube Channel or Instagram account?

Once you have a portfolio of high end listings, here's the fun part, grab a pen and paper.

1. Take your asset and cash-flow snapshot

Use a large sheet of paper on your table and write down all assets and its corresponding values, including Airbnb payout screenshots. On the second, draw a line down the middle and write down all incoming cash flow (Airbnb, VSBO dashboard and so forth) What is the property that creates stress and distraction without adding a lot of value?

2. SET A ONE MONTH MINI RETIREMENT IN ONE OF YOUR DESTINATIONS OVERSEAS

Choose a location with premium empty vacation home whether it is in Malta, Thailand or Australia. Show the prospective owner your portfolio and get it listed on Airbnb and VSBO.

3. AUTOMATE WITH THE THE AIRBNB EQUATION

Contact your team of VAs, think of setting a group chat on Slack, WhatsApp for one property. Get in touch with local cleaning agencies that bill you regularly and set up auto payment with credit cards that have reward points. Telling them to execute the system and give a trusted member of your family a free nights stay in one of your listings in Croatia, Tuscany or even Southern California.

> "For the past 33 years, I have looked in the mirror every morning and asked myself: If today were the last day of my life, would I want to do what I am about to do today?" And whenever the answer has been "No" for too many days in a row, I know I need to change something... Almost every thing- all external expectations, all pride, all fear of embarrassment or failure- these things just fall away in the face of death, leaving only what is truly important. Remembering that youa re going to die is the best way I know to avoid the trap of thinking you have something to lose."
> -Steve Jobs, College Dropout and CEO of Apple Computer, Stanford University Commencement, 2005.

Will 'bad things" happen while building my business? Yes, small problems are inevitable. Some of your guests might scratch one of the furnitures, turn it into a party house. But don't lose sight of the bigger picture, you will start that see that all business have problems so let the small bad things happen and make the bigger better things happen. Designing a lifestyle business requires massive action, your output. I challenge you to look at whatever you are doing and tell me what is the 20% of things you do that generate 80% of your outcome. We have far more control over our lives than many embrace.

In the past five years, of learning to say no to compulsively serving other people's needs to healing everyone's pain, to accepting all invitations. I finally came to realization that it is not helping me to reach my goals in life. It is easy for me to lose focus, to succumb to distraction until I started asking myself this question, is what I and doing now aligned with my life's calling? My calling or writing this book sharing this opportunity, lights me up and inspires me to share it with everyone. It has rewarded me socially, emotionally, and spiritually. At least I've found this renewed awareness of choice. The choice that I make in every moment counts.

And every day is an opportunity for you to create a living masterpiece. Life is either a daring adventure or nothing at all. Without disruption, entrepreneurs would not exist. Everyone have an ultimate goal in life, mine is to build a sustainable business. But most of us are too afraid to pursue it. Most people has an action bias but struggle to identify the problems that are causing the stress. I've found that getting clarity of what's wrong and why it's a problem is the best investment you can make at home or work.

The real work of an entrepreneur is with constant iteration, incorporating consumer feedback, troubleshooting and figuring out when to scale and when to limit losses. With cash flow and time, one day you will be designing a new business, and I hope it will change the world and make it better than the one we live in.

Fewer than 5% of the 195,000 books published each year sell more than 5,000 copies. I'd be really really surprised if this book can sell more than 1,000 copies. I decided not to reach any publishers to publish this book. All the writers by authors by Denis Johnson, Miranda July, David Foster Wallace or in the personal finance niche like Robert Kiyosaki, Dave Ramsay or George S. Clason. These are the writers who are in the top 1/1000 of 1% of writers. Writing for me is more of a spiritual practice as I spill the inside of myself and cleaning out the toxins which accumulated over the years of becoming an entrepreneur. If I don't write every day, I might lose the ability. And very soon, I might find myself detoxed and believe it or not, I'm making more like minded friends who read my book. So tell people something that nobody knows about you.

When I'm risking my every dime whether it is investing in the stock markets or building a portfolio of vacation properties, I've seen the bad the ugly and hopefully you won't repeat my mistakes. Remembering why you started this business will help you go through tough times. Lastly, picture in your mind that two years from now, finally generating that six figures passive income when the system is finally automated.

Most successful people I know have at lease one or two very strong opinions. Because no body in this world would care about all the things you don't have strong opinions on. Turn the world upside down, go explore the world and there are plenty of times you might find value where no-one else can see. The idea of Uber was born one winter night during the conference where the co founders were trying hard to get a cab in Paris attending an annual tech conference.

The tech giants like Uber and Airbnb did not generate this technological wave, but more than any other companies, they saw the wave and they surfed it and profited big from it. Airbnb can be considered the biggest hotel company on the planet and they are ultimately the twenty-first century internet business. Airbnb has taken age-old ideas, rent your home with new twists and indeed fostering a massive community of global travelers who had never previously existed.

Self publishing in this permission economy is the way to go. I don't need traditional publishers to tell me what cover designs to do, in fact, for less than $20 per month, I could create a book cover from canva.com with thousands of templates. I hate when I have to depend on other people choosing me, so I am now in full control of my contents and I can potential spread the message to thousands of people all around the world. Publishers will tell you they will help you do the marketing for your book, it is not true. I've talked to a lot of authors going through major publishing houses only to tell me they don't do any marketing at all. Even if they do, it's going to be minimal and ineffective. They are also layers of management to make decisions. But again, the industry is busy just surviving but fighting the wrong battles. Just look at taxi cab companies around the world doing the same fighting Uber to charge more for cabs. In a fair marketplace, I don't think anyone should control prices, but again, they are missing the point.

If you want to be an entrepreneur today, you don't need permission from your friends, parents or large corporations telling you that it's not possible. As an entrepreneur, artist, yoga teacher, traveller, doctor, you can now make money on the side, you will kick your competitors right in the butt and you will look amazingly cool at cocktail parties showing people you have a portfolio of cash generating properties. Pricing is not the priority, what you want is high distribution.

In reading this you have have the whole world open to you, and it has rolled the red carpet as you notice the wealth of opportunities to design a business with no inventories well and scale your business in a way that reaches hundreds if not thousands of travelers all around the world, which is they this is all about. If you publish a listing when the listing goes out. And if there is a disaster you can hold one, take the listing out and re-publish later, update without making a fuzz. You can move fast, because you are no large corporation with layers of bureaucracy.

Some people will be angry how fast technology is changing and its effect on traditional businesses. Some people will be angry as you capitalize on the current market changes. But most people will be grateful because you are delivering value with a cheaper alternative. Be that little boy in the Emperor Wears No Clothes. Go against all the previously set rules and don't accept the status quo. If you can't do that, don't be an entrepreneur.

It's the same for your listing on Airbnb, and it's true for this book, and that is why online stores like Amazon will reach the audience or make deals with others to give it away for free. I also wanted people to read the Airbnb Equation in a time where there is a big shift in the business world with technologies. I never wrote for money, but I did want readers. A well-crafted title of your listing also inspires confidence that the guest knows what they are getting. Airbnb has created a marketplace that has so little friction between you and potential customers, and with all the processing fees and distribution, they only take 3% from the money you make. It's massive because when we think that Uber is taking 25 percent per ride and it is outrageous. Very soon, they will be taking 100 percent as they roll out autonomous vehicles in the next three to five years.

Even in the publishing world, traditional publishers take about 85 percent of the profits per book sale when the largest publisher in the world, Amazon allows you self publish and they only take 30 percent of the profits. Amazon have provided authors or even bloggers the ability to publish their books within minutes.

> "It had long since come to my attention that people of accomplishment rarely sat back

and let thing happen to them. They went out and happened to things." Leonardo Da Vinci - Italian Renaissance polymath, painter of the Mona Lisa and The Last Supper.

CONCLUSION

A Monopolist is just a Rent Collector

In business, money is there an important thing or it is everything. In today flat global marketplace, it is easy to check what other businesses make on margins so you can plan for a long-term future. Just like what Peter Thiel, former *PayPal* Mafia coined the monopolist profits, the difference between the successful ones and the ones struggling to survive is monopoly profits.

Monopolist is just a rent collector and if you corner the market for something, you can jack up the price, and others will have no choice buy to buy it from you. The Airbnb equation could be the answer to 'no money down' of the 21st century.

The sharing economy at the time of this writing was created by some creative monopolists which created a market that never existed before. There is a lot of hype around new technologies like AI and the next wave of breakthrough technology. The property sector could face disruption with the rise of Artificial Intelligence and Virtual Reality. Real estate development will always be here and property and business ownership will not be replaced by AI because the values of properties are fixed all the time but the world we live in is dynamic.

But again, opportunists will be the one adapting and they drive progress because the promise of monopoly profits provides a powerful incentive to innovate. Airbnb or Uber invented something new and better which is good for the rest of society. Those are powerful marketplaces that is getting more users and getting better every day. Airbnb was the result for creating greater abundance and customers were happy to share their used properties to get

And for the rest of us, the question is how do we create cash flow from this shift? How do we capture profits over the next decade? It takes time to build something valuable and that can be accelerated with the help of technology, network effects and economies of scale and branding. You will still need to choose and market carefully and expand deliberately. Start with a very small market and expand to adjacent markets like the luxury short term rental market. When all the boxes are checked, you could be dominating a specific niche together with the discipline to expand gradually.

REFERENCES

- The Four Hour Work Week, Escape the 9-5, pg 36 live anywhere and join the new Rich— Tim Ferriss

-Homo Deus, A Brief History of Tomorrow Yuval Noah Harari

-Expert Secrets, The Underground Playbook, Russell Brunson

-Zero to One, Notes on Startups, or How to Build the Future, Peter Thiel

-Tribe of Mentor, Short life Advice from the best in the World, Timothy Ferriss

www.ingramcontent.com/pod-product-compliance
Lightning Source LLC
Chambersburg PA
CBHW030643220526
45463CB00004B/1626